CONFESSIONS
OF A FAILED SAINT

Terry Wilson

PARSE

ISBN-13: 978-1479279401
ISBN-10: 1479279404

PARSE

First Edition:
2013

TABLE OF CONTENTS

1

BECOMING A NUN,
LEPER, OR SAINT

When I was growing up, the one thing I knew would make my mother feel better was if I became a nun. "If only one of my kids would become "a religious," she'd say, and I took it on as my job. I have five brothers and sisters, and I'm the second youngest, the middle girl in the family. My older and younger sisters were way more perfect, but I was the one who needed to be sure my mother loved me.

My mother's sister was a nun, and sometimes we'd go and visit her at the convent where she lived. As soon as we walked into those hushed corridors with nuns scurrying around, my mother would say, "Now, look how nice their skin is! They really feed them well here!" Then at some point we'd end up in my aunt's room, a little cell with a hard, skinny twin bed and a pinewood dresser, and while my aunt was finishing up her prayers, my mother'd whisper to me, "This cell is really nice! You could have your own little cell if you lived here—look how clean it is!"

These trips to the convent were not convincing, but it was hard growing up Catholic—you could never get Jesus off the cross, for one thing. I needed clear signs to figure out whether I was a good person or not, but each day in school, there he was, still hanging in front of us, still bloody. "Your sins put him on the cross!" all the nuns and priests would tell us. Even when I knelt for 3 hours in church every Good Friday, even when I dragged myself out of bed and trudged to Mass in the snow on days I could have slept in, my parents still said I was "contrary."

No matter what I did, I couldn't be as holy as my two sisters or my three brothers were. Well, at least two of my brothers—my older brother Charley was the middle son, and he was a pain in the ass, according to my father, because he liked Elvis and wore his hair in a ducktail. Both of us were the black sheep of the family, and my father called us "hemorrhoids" when he got mad. But I thought Charley was cool.

Once when my father yelled at me, I ran upstairs to my bedroom and ripped the doily off the top of my dresser. Then, to punish my father, I grabbed a bobby pin, and carved my brother's favorite Elvis song into my cheap dresser top: "You ain't nothin' but a hound-dog, Crying all the time. You ain't never caught a rabbit, and you ain't no friend of mine!"

My father knew how to make everyone laugh though, including my mother. He used to tell those old jokes like, "What's that on the road, aHEAD?" When someone was boring, like my Uncle Monk who liked to stand on our dining room table and tell stories about his job at the doughnut factory, we never knew what my father would do. Sometimes he'd crawl out of the room on his hands and knees, and sometimes he'd get up out of his chair and slowly walk across the room. Then he'd let his pants fall down as though it was an accident. We thought that was the best thing ever, that my father could get away with this stuff. My mother yelled at him but we could tell she was trying not to smile.

I was like my father sometimes, so I got put in the corner at school for talking too much or for telling jokes in class. But I did give money to the Pagan Babies fund. When the nuns told us we could name the babies in Africa, I wanted to call them Zelda and Tiffany. "No, no, no," Sister said. "The only names we want to give to those poor children are Mary and Joseph, isn't that right, class?" And then she would smile, which meant we had no choice but to name all the people in Africa after the Holy Family.

In fourth grade I wrote in the three page autobiography we were assigned in class that I wanted to become a nun, but it was mostly because I wanted an A in the class. I wasn't sure about the convent because I knew I'd have trouble with the obedience part, so my next idea was, I'd become a leper.

Lepers, the nuns said, suffered like Jesus and sometimes they even lost parts of their bodies to the disease, for instance, their noses would fall off, but who cares; they'd go right to heaven! Plus, how could my father be mean enough to yell at me if I had leprosy? The only problem was, it was hard to catch leprosy in Buffalo. There I was, just getting used to myself without a nose, when I realized I'd have to go back to the nun idea.

Unless I could be a saint....Saints are really big in Catholicism. And not any old saint, just the ones who suffered really bad. In fact, we weren't that interested in the saint's life; I knew that my patron saint was St. Therese who when she died, let red roses fall down from heaven. Mostly we were interested in the saints' gruesome deaths.

One of my favorites was St. Sebastian who was tied to a tree and then 36 people shot arrows at his chest. He wasn't the same after that. Another in the Hall of Fame was St. Lucy who met up with someone who didn't like her and he actually tore her eyes out and then she carried them around on a dinner plate. St. Elmo, as it turned out, also had one bad day when he was on a boat and for some reason, he wasn't popular either. The other people on the boat hooked a huge winch into his stomach, and then they turned the crank and reeled in the rope until his intestines came out onto the deck. But all wasn't lost; he became the Patron Saint of Appendicitis.

These were my role models.

And I really appreciated their commitment. But maybe being a nun would be easier than having my eyes or intestines yanked out. Or I could be a missionary—my mother sent a dollar bill whenever she could to the Columban Missions and sometimes she'd talk about becoming a missionary herself, going off to Africa and saving those little kids without legs and arms there. I don't know why they had no legs or arms, but it seemed like my mother mostly talked about becoming a missionary when she was sick of us. For her, being a missionary was like taking a very long vacation to a foreign land where she wouldn't have to deal with six whiney kids and a husband who drank and gambled. But then she never went off to Africa, so I doubted I'd be able to either.

I had a best friend named Tricia and we did everything together for years, even started our own sorority. But one day she decided that she liked Carol Ann better than me and I wasn't her best friend anymore. I went home and told my mother; I was upset. My mother went into the kitchen and handed me one of those Columban Mission magazines with the amputee kids on the cover. She pointed at the picture.

"Be glad you have legs," she said.

Maybe that could be my new life's goal.

❖ ❖ ❖

2

CHICKEN

"**Y**our mother is your best friend!" my father bellowed at the kitchen table almost every night. He said this because he thought we didn't appreciate my mother enough. My mother meanwhile, cooking for eight people, served all of us first. Each of us was given a small piece of breast or a wing but my mother was always the last to sit down. When she did, there wasn't much left of the skinny little chicken plopped in the center of the table.

"I'll just eat the neck," she said, showing how to be a martyr in everyday life.

My father wouldn't tolerate my older brothers joking about anything my mother put on the table. She was an excellent cook, but making lunches for six kids on a policeman's salary, she had to cut some corners. My two oldest brothers were in high school and all they got for their midday meal was one slice of bologna trapped between two pieces of Wonder Bread.

"No one'll switch lunches with us in the cafeteria," Charley joked. "They say we eat air sandwiches."

"That's enough!" my father yelled, leaning forward with his red face. "Do you know how hard your mother works every day?" This was all true, but my real concern was that bird on its plated throne in the middle of the table. I kept my eye on its bony carcass because my father said the first one finished could pick the chicken.

Just then my sister Ann's elbow hit mine and I dropped my fork on the floor. She started to laugh.

"You poophead," I said, poking her with my elbow.

My father gave us a dirty look. "I called Our Lady of Victory Orphanage today, and I asked them if they'd like two little girls, Terry and Ann. They said we could trade you for two boys: Gussy and Ralph. Those boys are a lot more obedient than you are."

I wouldn't have minded getting rid of my sister Ann, but apparently it was a package deal: two of us for two of them. I kept my thoughts to myself and shoveled in the last of my potatoes. Although the orphanage might be glamorous with gloomy black outfitted saints wandering around and babies I could take care of.

"You kids," my father went on. "You don't appreciate anything! We give you food, clothing, and shelter, but do we ever get any thanks for it? No."

OK, we did have food, and I couldn't complain about still being hungry because my mother would say, "Just fix yourself a peanut butter sandwich and stop whining."

And the clothes, well, I had to wear my sister Mary's hand me downs and the armpits still smelled like her.

Shelter? I looked overhead at the cracked ceiling; I noticed the faded yellow curtains on the windows. Shelter, check.

What I really wanted though was the rest of that greasy chicken. I finished eating before Ann, and as soon as my father said the word, I'd descend on it like a vulture. My brother Bob was a poor eater; my older two brothers wanted to get away from the table. My older sister Mary was a martyr too, so the only one who'd fight me for it was Ann. I might give her one bone to gnaw on, but I'd get to eat the tiny bits of chicken left on skinny ribs, my prize for being patient, calculating, and still hungry.

❖ ❖ ❖

3

PROMISES

❦

I sat in the Holy Family Church pew under the domed ceiling with the Agony of Christ on Calvary portrayed above me and I listened to the priest. I was squeezed in again next to a fat woman in a mink coat, but this time I didn't mind. Because today was the day Father was going to tell us what the Blessed Mother had said to the three children at Fatima on that day long ago. I looked around as Father Menge entered the pulpit; the saints were waiting too, with their stone eyes that never blinked, waiting just as I was for that promise Mary had declared about the end of the world. Today was October 13, 1960, and the Pope had told the priests they could now share the contents of the sealed envelope that Lucia, the youngest of the children, had sent from her cloistered convent where she now lived as an adult.

I felt little as I knelt there, like I always did in Church. "Savior of the world!" the priest would loudly proclaim as he stood in front of the congregation at the end of the Mass each Sunday. "Save Russia!" the congregation would answer. The phrases about Communism's ending rang like church bells in my head as I anticipated Father Menge's revelation of Mary's secret. I knew Mary had spoken about the conversion of Russia in her first two vows, but she'd told the three children her last promise was more important than any of the others.

"And this is Mary's month," Father was saying now from the pulpit. He was about to tell us! I thought again of the fiery ball that came down to earth from heaven that day at Fatima, how God scared everyone away. Is that how the end of the world would be? The past two weeks at school we'd been going under the desks for air-raid drills. "In case of nuclear war, you'll be protected," Sister Scholastica told us confidently. As I walked to Church that morning, I'd thought of what would happen when the atom bomb from Russia hit us. I knew it'd be as fast as the traffic light that clicked at the corner of Tifft Street and South Park. Tick, boom, and my bones would be a shadow on the sidewalk, my frizzy hair a dusty imprint. I sure hoped Our Lady knew how to save us.

But at home, my mother was making goulash for dinner; my father was eating a creamy eclair with a glass of beer for breakfast. I wasn't sure why the rest of our family didn't worry about the Blessed Mother's vow like I did. My mother just said everything was God's will, and then she'd get a sad look on her face like she never expected any good news to come from anywhere. But the Blessed Virgin Mary could rescue us even if there were Communists in the world. She was kinder than God the Father. She wouldn't let the world end when I was only nine.

Father Menge was droning on now about the Rosary and Altar Society and I thought about other promises the Church made. Usually the bad ones came true, like if you ate meat on Friday and died right afterwards, you'd go to hell, unless you said a perfect Act of Contrition just after the truck hit you and just before you landed on the pavement and died. I shifted in my seat, wishing the lace on my dress wasn't stuck to my legs. It was the good promises I wasn't sure about. I thought of my father throwing up blood in the bathroom on the day he was supposed to take me to the Father-Daughter breakfast at Holy Family. My mother said he was sick and I needed to be a very good girl. Then we didn't talk about it. Often my father would assure my mother, "Tomorrow I quit drinking," and I'd be listening at the top of the stairs, happy that my real father was coming back. Till the next day when he came shambling in the front door again with guilty, bleary eyes, and I'd wonder if I'd upset him somehow.

"Thanks be to God!" the congregation cried as Father finished and came down from the pulpit. Had I missed the secret promise? Or had God and the Pope decided not to tell us? I looked up at the ceiling again and at the stained glass windows all around us: Jesus suffering in the Garden of Gethsemane, Jesus being whipped, Jesus being dragged up the hill where he'd be hung on the cross. Mary stood on her altar, just a big piece of rock like the rest of the statues and suddenly I felt her promise slipping away like the incense smoke that floated above us. And I knew that nothing would change, after all.

❖ ❖ ❖

4

HOLY CARDS

Sometimes for Valentine's Day at Holy Family School, we'd get holycards. I knew at public schools, the boys gave the girls valentines that said "U-R-4-ME" on the front and had a heart with the boy's name on the back. But in Catholic school, most of us gave each other holycards, instead. Sister liked it better; she said that valentines made unpopular kids feel bad because they never got any.

But the holycards made me feel bad. On the front, there would be Mary, looking holy in a white gown, or the Infant of Prague, standing on top of the globe like a brat. There were so many saints, and they all had blood gushing out of them: St. Elmo, St. Sebastian, St. Lucy, St. Agnes, St. Cecilia—I felt like I knew the whole tormented gang. Jesus had his own cards, too: Jesus in anguish. Like the one with his Sacred Heart pierced and blood spilling out. Never did I see a holycard with Jesus having fun—Jesus on a date or at a barbecue. Yet Jesus' Sacred Heart bleeding was a popular picture: the enlarged version hung in the front hall at our house.

The worst thing about getting a holycard instead of a valentine on Valentine's Day was that if you turned over the holycard, sometimes there was "In Memoriam" on the back to someone who had died. During funerals, they always gave out holycards with a prayer on the back for the dead person. It wasn't so bad getting one of these at a funeral home; in fact, growing up, it always seemed someone on our street was dying. I had to go to the wake and look at him in the casket.

"Doesn't he look good?" my mother would ask. The flowers were white and yellow and smelled like death, but I got quite a collection of holycards. I saved all the different saints just like my brother saved baseball cards.

We decided to put our funeral home visitation to good use. We'd grab a handful of the holycards when the family wasn't looking and it saved us a lot of money on valentines. We'd just sign our name under the tortured saint in our perfect slant and ovals handwriting. I didn't mind giving the holycards but I sure hated getting them.

Then one year in fourth grade, my friend Pat said that Matthew Peterson liked me. I was thrilled; he was much more handsome than Anthony Ruggiero, my second grade flame. Plus, Matthew was rich. His father was a dentist and they had a summer home on the lake. Matthew was two rows away from me because his last name started with "P" and sometimes we looked at each other and smiled.

Valentine's Day came that year and I prepared my supply of memorial holycards the night before. It still was important how many holycards you got, even if it wasn't romantic. I came to school that morning with my shopping bag full and I knew I'd give a card to Matthew, but I hadn't decided what to write on it yet. He came up to me first, though, in the schoolyard and handed me a flat, square box. "Happy Valentine's Day," he mumbled and looked embarrassed. Then the bell rang and everyone was lining up. I didn't want the class to see what it was, so I hid it in my bookbag.

It was hard to wait until lunch to see what he'd given me but I knew how Sister would get if she thought something funny was going on between Matthew and me. She thought girls should go into the convent. When the bell for lunch rang, I took my bookbag into the girls' lavatory and took out the white box. It was plain on the outside, but when I opened it, inside was a large red paper heart, folded. I had to use both hands to open it wide and hook it in the back, and it had an arrow going through it. "To Terry," one side of the arrow said. "Love, Matthew," was on the other side.

Wow. I'd never gotten such a beautiful valentine before and never had any boy told me he loved me. I knew Saint Valentine was holy, too, but I didn't want a picture of him. I was happy to celebrate Valentine's Day in a new way. As I left the bathroom, I felt all the suffering saints smiling down on me.

❖ ❖ ❖

5

CONFESSION

One night in Girl Scouts, something in me turned bad. Our meetings were held in the Presbyterian Church basement; Miss Pat and Miss Mary were our leaders. All the girls on our street were there, too: Roseanne Noshodly with the big nose; bratty Carol Ann Kingsley who had long curls like mine; my best friend, Pat Hines; Nancy Dicklan who was shy; and Peggy Sperditi, who was very sophisticated. Peggy's mother talked to her about important, secret things and Peggy had a padded bra. We respected her for that. The older scouts were talking about badge projects with the leaders on the other side of the room so they weren't paying attention to us.

Peggy said she had something big to tell us. We thought it was gossip about Miss Pat who wasn't married yet. We gathered around her in the far corner of the basement and sat on the steps leading up to the sanctuary.

"I know about the birds and the bees," Peggy began. "My mother told me all about it and she said not to tell you because your mothers might get mad."

I was scared to hear what she had to say, but I was also very interested. My mother was embarrassed if I even saw her in her slip.

"It's sex," Peggy continued.

Suddenly, I knew what Peggy was about to tell us was a sin. Wasn't that the reason Saint Maria Goretti was murdered, because she wouldn't commit the sin of sex? That's what the nuns told us.

"Hurry up and say it!" Pat whispered loudly to Peggy. "Miss Pat will be coming over here in a few minutes!" I decided to listen to the rest. I wanted to be pure but I was almost eleven and I was curious. Besides, all the other girls were listening and they saw Jesus die on the cross for their sins every day at Holy Family School, just like I did.

Peggy looked smug. "Well, you know that hole where you pee? The man gets on top of the lady and puts his thing inside her hole and babies get made. It even hurts sometimes," she finished.

Roseanne screamed. "You're lying!"

"No, I'm not," Peggy declared. "Once I peeked into my parents' bedroom and saw them rolling around, so I know it's true."

"It sounds sickening," Pat said. Carol Ann was crying. Miss Pat walked toward us then so I said nothing. But I felt something breaking inside of me. How could Peggy's claim be true? And if it was, I shouldn't have stayed to listen.

About two weeks later, Roseanne told her busybody mother and she ended up telling all our parents that we knew the "facts of life." Soon afterwards, my parents called me into the living room "to talk." My family never had "talks." I tried to block out what Peggy had told us that night but as soon as I got to the living room and saw my father sitting in the green armchair with that angry look on his face, I had an idea what we'd be talking about.

"Why did you listen to that Sperditi girl?" my father yelled. "She's got no business telling you that trash." I squirmed and looked at the enlarged picture of the Blessed Mother ascending into heaven on our living room wall. "What's wrong with you, hearing that dirty talk? That's a sin against the sixth commandment!"

I looked at my feet and realized they'd never be ascending into heaven.

Neither would the rest of me. "Sex is sacred!" my father whispered in a hard, menacing voice.

"She's not going to talk about it anymore, are you, Terry?" My mother reassured my father, trying to calm him down. "If you have a question to ask sometime, you can ask me," my mother told me, "but really, little girls shouldn't be thinking about such things."

I blocked out the whole issue of sex for about two days but then questions started coming into my mind. I kept asking my mother questions like, "Mom, how many kids can a lady have?" My mother would answer, "As many as God wants her to have," as she hurried out of the room. One night I was babysitting next door at the Andol's and as I held the very young baby, I visualized it being inside Mrs. Andol's body. I wondered if Mr. Andol could have sex with her while the baby was growing inside. I called my mother on the phone to ask her and she said she'd talk to me about it when I got home, but that I was asking too many questions.

I came up the porch stairs when I arrived home at midnight from babysitting, hoping my mother would be up and we could talk and have hot chocolate. When I came in the door, though, the house was dark and I noticed my father's coat on the coat rack. As I came up the stairs, I saw a sliver of light from the door to my parents' room and suddenly a huge voice boomed out, "STOP THINKING ABOUT SEX! YOU'RE ANTICIPATING MARRIAGE AND IT'S A MORTAL SIN!" I froze on the step, paralyzed. I knew it was my father yelling at me, but it seemed like God.

After that, I couldn't stop thinking about sex. The more I tried to block out visions of naked men and women doing it, the more they popped uncontrollably into my mind. My mother had told my father on me, so I knew I couldn't ask her any more questions about my thoughts. I felt like I shouldn't even go to Communion after that even though I still had to go to Church on Sundays and holydays. I didn't feel close to God at all. God the Father reminded me of my father when he was angry; God the Father had never liked me. I knew God the Son was probably disgusted with me. The Holy Ghost who looked like a parakeet was the only one left and I was sure he'd flown away from my impure mind.

I started going to Confession every day that year. At Holy Family Church, no one noticed because there were so many priests who worked there and none of them really knew me or cared what I did. I never felt clean, though, no matter how many times I confessed, because as soon as I closed the confessional door to say my penance, the bad thoughts came into my mind again. I'd have to start counting them right away for my next confession. I became obsessed with sinning that year; everything seemed like a sin. It was my last year of grammar school and we had our one and only sex education class in the auditorium, but I hardly listened. It was only a movie anyway and the film projector kept breaking every time the sperm or eggs came onto the screen. Sister Aurelia was too embarrassed to answer any questions and besides, the boys were outside the auditorium making faces at us through the window.

The next time I got a cold, I wondered if I had been using too much toilet paper at school to blow my nose. That could be a sin of stealing, I thought, and decided to ask my mother. She seemed surprised that I was worrying, then laughed and said I was being too "scrupulous." It didn't seem funny to me that I was so tortured but I looked up the word "scrupulous" in the dictionary and it said, "very conscientious and exacting, having scruples." I thought I was supposed to be using my conscience; that's what the Baltimore Catechism told us.

When I was twelve, I started to bleed one day but I didn't want to tell my mother because I was embarrassed and ashamed it was my fault that my insides were coming out. For two days, I put toilet paper in my underpants and wondered if I was dying. Finally, I told my mother and she marched me up to the bathroom and gave me a pamphlet to read about sanitary napkins and belts.

I entered high school when I was thirteen. Before the first week was out, I found out where the chapel was so I could go to confession there as soon as possible. I began telling my sins to Father O'Brien, an old Irish priest with a brogue like my grandmother. He had a shamrock on his jacket and he always smiled at me. I was glad there was a screen in the confessional to shield my face; I knew he wouldn't be smiling at an immodest girl otherwise. Finally, after about two weeks of going to confession and telling my bad thoughts almost every day, Father O'Brien asked me to meet him after school in his rectory office; he wanted to talk to me.

I was scared to talk to a priest in person about these thoughts I'd been tormented with for a year and a half. Except for telling them in confession anonymously, I hadn't had to admit I was having them to anyone. I didn't tell Father O'Brien the whole story but he knew about my impure thoughts.

"Am I just plain bad?" I asked him as he sat behind his desk with his balding head and his big stomach. He smiled at me and took my hand.

"It's the devil tempting you," he told me. "The devil is making you think these thoughts. You mustn't blame yourself, child."

I was so relieved I started to cry; that was the first time anyone said my sins weren't my fault. When I left Father O'Brien's office, I felt clean again, at least for a little while.

6

BAD CHRISTMASES

"You have a whole new lucky life," my friend Kim told me that Christmas of 1988 when I was still living in Los Angeles. I had a new job I liked, a new lover, and my roommate's cat had just been de-flead. But three days before Christmas as I sat on the edge of my bed, I got a phone call.

"Liz Marek is dead," my friend said.

"No way!" I yelled. "Liz? It has to be a mistake!"

"It's true," my friend said, her voice catching. "She was in that plane they shot down over Scotland—Pan Am 103."

Over the next few days, the news blazed with stories of the fireball that lit up the sky in Lockerbie, Scotland, but the only thing stuck in my mind was how Liz's lonely remains lay in the snow thousands of miles away. How could it be? Liz was my friend in acting class, much better at improvisation than I was. Liz, the trombone player in the Cherry Cokes, the lead singer in her leather jacket when they played "Leader of the Pack." Liz, giggling next to me as we watched Pee Wee Herman's Big Adventure, Liz who traveled to the mountains in Idyllwild with me, both of us joking about our Catholic childhoods as we hiked but Liz still modest in the hotel room as she undressed, her white flabby legs lit up by the moon outside the window. And now she was gone.

I exchanged Christmas gifts with my lover that year, and we'd already bought and decorated the tree, but I felt like someone was standing on my chest because Liz was still on that cold hillside and I'd never see her again.

Another Christmas, I think it was 1986, I decided I needed to help others. I'm too self-centered; that's why Christmas is depressing me, I thought. I talked my friend Marty into going with me to serve breakfast at 6 am. on Christmas morning at the Rescue Mission in downtown LA. We arrived before dawn even broke and we were given our duties: I was in charge of oatmeal and Marty's job was doughnut delivery. Someone else's mission was the scrambled eggs. While the men lined up, all scruffy and smelling of alcohol with a few days' or weeks' growth of beard on them and I slopped overflowing ladles of oatmeal onto their paper plates, Marty plopped the doughnuts at the edge, and the egg lady slid scrambled gook next to the oatmeal. The men shuffled away, each finding himself a chair and then Marty poured coffee into Styrofoam cups and handed them each one. For three hours we slopped, plopped, and poured and didn't look at each other because I knew Marty's mother had been a drunk who tried to hang herself in the garage every other day, Marty being the one who would stop her before she kicked the chair away. And my father had been the Irish drinker cop who screamed at me with the same bloodshot eyes we both saw in every man sitting in that room, stuffing eggs in their mouths with their fingers, oatmeal caked in their beards.

Later, as we walked out the door, three hours of charity under our belts, I finally looked at Marty as the rain pelted the oil-slicked streets. "Let's kill ourselves," he said.

The next Christmas I thought, OK, I've learned my lesson. No alcoholics this year. I'll help different people, get my mind off myself. This was the option that occurred to me, after being raised Catholic. I'd spent years as a kid and teenager visiting the elderly in nursing homes, their heads lolling to the side as they sat in straight-backed wooden wheelchairs in a line along the wall. People in jails, people in hospitals—saving them all sounded reasonable. So in 1990, this became my plan in spite of my unsatisfactory experience the year before. I joined up with the Hunger Project and they almost convinced me how we'd cure the world of hunger but on the way, we'd stop off at the Juvenile Detention Center on Christmas day: bring them gifts, sing carols and generally cheer them up so much they'd forget they were in jail for the holidays.

We piled onto the bus Christmas morning, another drizzly one in LA, and Eric, the leader of the group, spoke in a loud voice how great it was that we were going—some of these kids had no visitors at all, much less visitors on Christmas, much less visitors who brought them gifts and sang to them! I listened, though a niggling voice inside me pricked at my "Peace on earth, good will to men" demeanor. "Come on!" I told myself. "Get in the Christmas spirit!" We tumbled out of the bus onto the asphalt parking lot of the Detention Center, humming Christmas carols and laden with bags and boxes of surprises until we were stopped at the door by the guards—and their metal detectors.

"Gotta check everyone," they yelled as we lined up. "No contraband allowed." The metal detectors beeped when they got to my underwire bra but I didn't feel like explaining this to the guard. Our gifts were wrapped for the boys but the guards were the ones who opened them, deciding which we should give the residents. No combs with long handles were allowed, could be stuck in someone's eye. No hardcover books, could be used as a chest shield. No candy or sweets, made the boys too hyper. Only soap, crossword puzzles, and Hardy Boys mysteries made it through, all of which seemed less fun without the red and green paper, ribbons now on the floor.

The boys were brought out and some seemed to appreciate any gift given to them, but most watched us through slit eyes as we sang, "Tis the season to be jolly, fa la la la la, la la la la." Finally we left, Eric giving them the Peace sign as he walked out the door, but before I got on the bus, I glanced back at the window to see three kids giving us a different kind of sign—their middle finger. "I think we really helped them today," Eric was saying as I pulled myself onto the bus.

A Christmas that started out badly but ended up better was when I was 8 years old. I had to sit on the couch after

Christmas Mass and be good in my red and green polyester dress while my mother served eggnog and cookies to as many nuns and priests who could fit into our living room. My mother pretended our family was normal even though my father often did strange things if he'd had too many Genesee beers. Lucky for my mother that day, he was working, but actually my sister Ann and I were hoping for an end to our boredom and having to smile when my aunt, also a nun in a severe black habit, gave us all the presents she'd gotten as tokens of appreciation for being principal of St. Martin's School—gifts she didn't want, like black rubber boots. My mother told us we had to be thankful for these even though what we really coveted was the nun candy my aunt only brought one box of, to share with us.

"Do you know how many Whitman's Samplers I got this year?" my aunt would laugh, and I'd think, *Keep the boots; give us the chocolate!* But still we had to try on the galoshes at least, say how warm they'd be even if they were three sizes too big, or smell the Nivea skin cream we'd also gotten, nun cream, rub it into our hands and say how nice it was. But this one Christmas turned out to be different. Because as the gifts were opened and the nuns and priests sipped their drinks, I looked up from my perch on the couch and noticed that three big starlings were flying down our stairwell and about to zoom in for a landing in our living room! I elbowed Ann, realizing they'd slipped in through a hole in our chimney, and all of a sudden, there they were, careening through the living room. The nuns and priests started screaming and my saintly grandmother, afraid they'd nest in our hair, yelped, "Put a lampshade on your head!" Ann and I yelled too and I tried to catch them and finally they flew out the front door but by then, I was laughing so hard I couldn't stop, and that was the best Christmas I ever had.

❖ ❖ ❖

7

DIVINE MUD

7/03/14

About twenty years ago when I first moved to Santa Fe, I lived in a big house off Highway 14, down a long dirt road that turned into a nightmare of clinging goo when the rains came in the spring. This same problem arose in the winter when the snow melted too fast; our cars got stuck on that 2 1/2 mile road. I lived with a wealthy woman in a huge house at the end of the road, a house she owned and ran as a bed and breakfast.

She had her idiosyncrasies—she vacuumed every day, and she got angry if even one of my curly hairs fell on her immaculate tile floor. If her ex-husband visited and tracked mud in on his feet, she wouldn't speak to him for days. But she especially hated our neighbor, Joe, because he had only one leg and shot his gun off each night at random times. Also, he owned at least 17 junker cars that he kept on his property. She filed a formal complaint and planned on meeting him in court. He didn't have the cars on her property, but she felt his junkers were ruining the neighborhood and she was trying to run a business. I saw her point, but the truth was, Joe was friendly, and she wasn't. I always waved at him, sitting on his stoop when I passed on my walks down that long road.

One January night, about 10 inches of snow fell on Santa Fe. It was pretty for a few days, but then the weather warmed up to almost 50 degrees. The snow melted quickly, and the road turned from clay to soup almost overnight. How was I going to get to work?

I had a friend in town named Carol, and she had a huge Ford pick-up she called "Old Whitey."

"Any chance I could borrow Old Whitey to get down my road for a few days?" I asked her. The snow in town had pretty much melted, so she didn't need her 4-wheel drive. "You can use my Honda."

"OK," she said. "But be careful of the power steering; I just got it fixed."

After she and I switched vehicles that Sunday morning, I'd headed toward Unity Church for the first time so I could beef up my spirituality for the week. I got dressed up because you never knew who you'd run into. Rumor had it that there were some hunky guys lurking around, so I wore my long Western skirt and matching top, plus my best red leather cowboy boots. They were pointy and shiny and my only fancy footwear. I also wore my most long and dangly earrings.

As I walked into church, I saw a mirror in the hallway. I couldn't resist checking myself out when I noticed the inscription below it: "Behold God." Awesome! Unfortunately, I didn't meet any buffed guys, except for the minister himself. He had beautiful dark eyes; plus he looked like he worked out. His name was Reverend Dave, but if I squinted, he reminded me of George Clooney.

The service ended around noon, and afterwards I bought two bags full of groceries and other provisions from Wild Oats. I'm generally an optimistic person, so I pointed Old Whitey toward home, thinking that the afternoon sun had not gotten hot enough yet that day to melt our icy road and I'd be able to traverse it without sinking into the mud. *Be positive!* Reverend Dave had repeated.

After traveling about fifteen miles south of the city, I reached the head of our road. As Carol had instructed me, I pulled the truck over and got out, then crouched down and rotated some gadget on the front tires to put the pickup into four-wheel drive. I was set! By then it was after one pm. *The Divine Mind is in everything*, the handsome minister had said. I took a deep breath and forged ahead.

I started off speeding, thinking that the faster I could get down the road, the better. Within moments, though, the truck slowed to a crawl as the clay instantly accumulated on the tires, its thick brown goop making the wheels of the car more and more gigantic. *Step on the gas; you can do this!* I told myself. The engine revved up and I skidded left and right as huge chunks of pudding flew up around the pickup and began sticking to the white body, but especially to the windshield. I was not only completely out of control; I could barely see! Old Whitey was sinking in the soupy ruts, journeying down, down, to the center of the earth. I struggled to turn the steering wheel but I needed more muscles. Inch by inch, the truck was slurping along in the goop, and then the steering wheel froze in place.

Shit! Where is the damn Divine Mind when you need it? I was about a mile and a half down the road and the truck was rooted to the ground— not moving one more inch on its own. Now what? I sat there for a moment, considering my options. Can I possibly walk home? I weigh a lot less than Old Whitey. If I walk softly...I opened the door and stuck the pointy toe of my shiny boot in the mud. I put a little weight on it. Dammit! My boot vanished into the muck! I pulled it back out, trying to shake the mud off of it, then tried to wipe it off with a bunch of Kleenex.

"Help!" I yelled. I couldn't ruin my only pair of red cowboy boots! I looked around and saw that I was still almost a mile from our house. How was I supposed to walk all that way when the mud was like glue? I sat there again for a minute, then decided I'd have to trudge home somehow. The truck door was still open, so I grabbed one of my bags of groceries, the one that apparently contained some spilled soup from Wild Oats deli counter. The paper bag unceremoniously ripped open from the soup and two of my grapefruits rolled out into the mud. "Help!" I yelled again.

As it turned out, the truck had gotten stuck very close to Joe's rickety trailer and junk car farm. I couldn't believe it when our neighbor opened his door and yelled back. "I'll save you!!" he said, standing on his front step with his one good limb. He'd told me once when I asked him how he lost his leg, "Well, I was really drunk one night, and I just fell over and bit my own leg. Got the gangrene, had to have it chopped off."

But at the moment, he was hopping over to one of his old beater cars. "I'll tow you!" he yelled, but the car he'd gotten into didn't start. He hopped over to another one and it fired right up. But he rolled down the window and shouted, "This sucker only goes backwards!" I sat in Old Whitey in amazement. *You never know what form your savior will take*, the minister had said.

Joe had to back up almost to my truck, then maneuver the junk heap around so he was still backwards on the road to my house and could pull me. When the front of his car was a foot or two from the front of my truck, he somehow jumped out, got some rope out of his trunk, and managed to tie the two vehicles together. I'd gotten halfway out of the truck, so it would seem like I was helping even if I wasn't. My butt still sat on the edge of the driver's seat, but at least I was in solidarity with him: one leg in the mud.

Did he fly? Did he hover? I swear I don't remember exactly how it all came about. It's possible that he was really Moses, parting the Red Sea of mud. I knew I had witnessed some kind of miracle.

Once the vehicles were joined together, we got back into them and he laboriously towed me home.

"Thanks!" I shouted when we got to my house, but he

was busy trying to turn his car around again.

My red boots were never the same after that. And neither was Old Whitey; I had to pay for her to get new power steering.. My housemate also had a fit about my muddy boots entering her spotless house that day. She kept up her campaign against our neighbor, but I knew after that, Joe was some kind of angel, the type who packed heat. Each night after that, when he shot his gun off into the starry sky, I cheered him on.

❖ ❖ ❖

8

RECIPE FOR EGGS THERESE

●

I have been single on and off in my life, which has necessitated a familiarity with household duties. But in my 54 years, I can honestly say that I've gotten away with as little cooking as possible. I mean, who wants to take the time when you're hungry? Who wants to dirty all those dishes? And most importantly, who wants to eat what I cook?

Not even me. So I may as well make my concoctions simple, low cal, and use as few dishes as possible. That's why in the following recipes, you'll notice a lot of boiling going on. Because boiling has the distinct advantage of using only one pan. Plus, I'm of Irish descent and God knows the Irish have never been known for their gourmet meals. I think the reason the Irish are still around, considering the English have been trying to kill them off for 700 years, is because boiling is much more low cal and healthy than all that oil that the Italians use and all the cheese that the French like so much.

But I digress. My favorite meal used to be poached eggs on spinach with popcorn on the side, which I remember creating when I lived in LA in a garage apartment before I started taking antidepressants. In fact, I don't think I've made this meal since I've been on antidepressants. What is the effect of poached eggs and popcorn on serotonin levels? I don't think Dr. Weil has explored this arena.

Actually, eggs seem to be a staple of this bachelorette diet. Which makes it all the more surprising that I've never learned to cook eggs in a way that tastes good. Kind of sad when you think about it.

So there I was yesterday, Mark, out of town again, working, and the Sunday before he left, he'd made me a very yummy scrambled egg, spinach, and onion combo for breakfast. Who needs him? I thought. Why can't I cook this egg combo myself?

I offer the following directions so you can experience the exquisite pleasure I had yesterday when I made my own Sunday egg extravaganza, or as I like to call it, "Eggs Therese."

1. Find whatever is in the refrigerator and hope that you have at least one white onion, plus a handful of spinach and two eggs that haven't been in the fridge too long. Make sure that the eggs have no Easter egg coloring on them because these would be the eggs we hardboiled last spring.

2. Chop up the onion as quickly as possible so that smell

doesn't make you cry. Crying is good in therapy and I'm all for it, but if you wipe your eyes with the hand that caressed the onion, you'll be weeping all day. You'll probably remember that you don't like chopping and you never dice, so you throw whatever pieces you managed to hack off the onion already, into the nearest frying pan. Then if the frying pan is small enough and you can't find a lid for it, put the teapot over it so those smelly onions don't stink up the whole house.

3. Open all the doors in the house and let those suckers cook for awhile.

4. Go outside and get the Sunday paper and hope that it hasn't been thrown into the road by the delivery person like it was yesterday when fourteen cars ran over it and you only had news confetti to read.

5. Pull the purple beach chair out of your trunk and get settled on the porch for a nice breakfast. Breakfast! Run back into the house and check on the onions. Yes, still cooking under the teapot. Still smelly.

6. Grab that handful of spinach and throw it in the frying pan. Mush it around a little.

7. Feed the cat, empty the kitty litter, take out the garbage, water the plants...until you hear that crackling sound. This means the onions are done.

8. Lift the teapot and see what happened. You may notice the

onions are now black, and think, this can't be good. You may also notice that the spinach and onions have now congealed into what looks like one disgusting cookie. If your next thought is, Wow, I know what this combo needs—two eggs! Then you're on the right track.

9. Break the two eggs into the mixture and notice that they don't mingle in because the onions and spinach are now a continent unto themselves. Be fearless and stab the continent with a knife until the eggs start to seep in. Remember then that you should never use silverware with Teflon, so get a pink plastic fork out of the drawer and stab some more. Notice one prong is now missing from the plastic fork. Find it and pluck it out. Replace the teapot so Eggs Therese can now simmer, or at least blister.

10. Read the front page on the porch in your beach chair and pretend it's the weekend before when your honey was cooking and you could smell those delectable eggs.....eggs! Run back into the kitchen, and smell....the bottom of the teapot burning? Remove it without delay. Turn off the fire.

11. Gaze upon your breakfast, now a large, yellow, black, and green coaster. Appreciate that you can pick the whole thing up in one piece with a fork. Slide it onto a plate and hope that your partner comes back before next Sunday's breakfast.

✤ ✤ ✤

9

MEETING AND MARRYING MARK

Many years ago, sometime between the last Ice Age and the year I began my first stable relationship, I sat in my doctor's office one day. I was there for a routine checkup and out of boredom, picked up an old copy of Field and Stream. To my amazement, there was an article that said the best way to meet guys was to join a fly-fishing class. I had no fishing rod and I hate flies, but at the time it had been a couple years since my last relationship, and that article got me thinking. I decided if fishing wasn't for me, maybe I should learn Contra dancing which is kind of a cross between Country western and square dancing. Now I can hold my own in a bar doing Disco, but I'm a free spirit, so I don't do well with steps. Still, I thought, why not try something new? Besides they gave lessons at this place.

So off I went to the Oddfellows Hall on Cerrillos Road — the name should have given me a clue. I walked in, wearing my long skirt and best rayon blouse, and right away, I saw this woman about 50 yrs. old in the middle of the dance floor, giving instructions. She was small and perfect, with lots of makeup on and her red hair pouffed up. She wore the requisite cowboy blouse with double pockets and a long broomstick skirt and Concho belt, with cowboy boots, and she was even bossier than Sister Gaudentia, my elementary school principal.

"OK, everyone, get on the floor. Grab a partner. Turn your partner. Do si do! Allemande right! Flip your partner over your head! Star left! Bow to your corner! Slam your partner against the wall!"

First of all, I had no partner. Then a guy who looked like he was 85 came up to me and held out his hand. I couldn't help but wonder if he was up to it, but it turned out I was the one who wasn't up to it. "Turn! Swing! Allemande left! Toss your partner out the door!"

I stepped on the poor guy's feet about seventy times. After forty minutes, I had to leave because my neck was killing me. I couldn't turn it to the left or right and my back was completely in spasm. I had to go home and put ice on my neck, then sit in a hot bath of Epsom salts and see my chiropractor the next day.

I decided to take a break from trying to meet guys; I was only 48, after all. Maybe I could still go into the convent and at least make my mother happy. At that point, my close friend Judy was getting married, and she asked me to be her

Maid of Honor. I've always hated weddings because they made me feel lonely. All through my childhood and young adulthood, I had to attend or be part of my two sisters' weddings, plus countless cousins, nieces, and nephews. But I told Judy that I would do it; I couldn't turn her down. ❦

The day of the wedding came, and I woke up grumpy. It was a cloudy afternoon in August, and I had to get all dressed up and drive my butt to Holy Ghost campground out past Glorieta. I ended up hitching a ride with another friend of mine, which was lucky because he had a jeep and the road was a series of huge potholes. But the ceremony turned out nice and sentimental and I was feeling a little less dismal when I approached the food table.

"Hi!" a tall good-looking guy walked up to join me. "Come here often?" I laughed and we introduced ourselves; then after we ate together, I talked him into dancing with me since there was disco playing, and he didn't look like an Oddfellow. Mark ended up taking me for a ride in his mid-life crisis white rental convertible, and over a period of hours, we didn't run out of things to talk about. While we watched the sunset, he kissed my hand.

Much later that evening, after a special dinner with the bride and groom where I found out he was divorced but had been friends of the groom for 30 years, Mark and I pulled up in front of my funky adobe house. Decision time—should I invite him in? Should I get involved with this guy who actually lived in Baltimore—a long distance relationship? But he traveled with his job and he was a sweetheart...plus he was tall...I liked that...

"Can I come in and meet your cats?" he said. It was either a great pick-up line or he loved cats, so I gave in.

"Can you wait outside five minutes?" I said, leaving him in his convertible, listening to Tchaikovsky in the warm night air. I ran into the little adobe. Since I had no clothes dryer, my just-washed sheets were hanging from the rickety chandelier in the living room. My underpants were dangling from the exercise bike and from both ends of the TV antenna. I pulled down the sheets, scooped up all the underwear, and threw everything into the bedroom, including all the unpaid bills and circulars on my tiny kitchen table. I unhooked the dripping hose of the washer from the sink and rolled that whole contraption into the bedroom too, and just as I shut the door, I heard Mark knocking at the front. Luckily we didn't sleep together that night because we couldn't have gotten into the bedroom, but we found out we really liked each other's kisses, and I fell in love with the smell of his neck.

We talked on the phone every day for a month after that, and got to know each other pretty well. Plus, he sent me yellow roses often. Finally, a month later, he came to visit, and this time when he knocked at the front door, the sheets weren't hanging from the chandelier— which was good because as soon as he walked in, we fell into each other's arms and kissed for 90 minutes straight—it was a kissing vortex.

Mark and I had a long-distance relationship for two years, and then he moved to Santa Fe and we began living together. Two years later, he had to work in Australia and right near Uluru, the sacred rock of the Aborigines, we got engaged. Mark is a joy; one image I keep in my mind is a time we were on a beach and there were many birds around. Mark kept feeding them tiny bits of bread and they came closer and closer, then finally he placed the crumbs on his outstretched arms and the birds landed on his hands, his arms, his shoulders. Maybe he is St. Francis reincarnated, I don't know. 🐦

While Mark and I were engaged, I got a little nervous about commitment. I wasn't going to be a runaway bride, but there are generations of expectations for the bride-to-be, even if I was over 50 and it was my first marriage. As a little girl, every time a flock of birds flew overhead, we'd all look up and say, "My wedding!" Thus reserving that group of sparrows for the big day and hoping they put the date in their appointment books. The first order of business, buying a wedding gown, proved daunting, partly because the first stop I made was a Bridal Shoppe downtown that was so classy, it didn't even have its name on the front. Judy was helping me with my wedding dress quest, since she was going to be my Maid of Honor. "I've been looking at Bridal Magazines all my life," she told me on the way over, which made me more anxious.

The funny thing was, I hadn't so much as worn a skirt the whole six months beforehand because of a knee surgery. The ugly, orthopedic Z-coils I had to wear were incompatible with everything but jeans. I had them on that day, of course, and by the time we got into the dressing room, the heavy set woman who was about to help me put on a very fancy, white corseted wedding dress with a train, took one horrified look at the heavy, brown orthopedics I'd just taken off and then proceeded to accidentally drop an entire box of straight pins into my shoes.

"Sorry!" she said, then peered at me. "Are you wearing makeup?" I thought it was kind of obvious that I had lipstick on, but I said yes.

"Then you have to wear this mesh bag over your head and zip it each time we put a dress on you or take a dress off," she said. "We can't get makeup on the dresses."

"OK," I said, and she handed me the white hood which I inserted my head into. Then she began to put the gigantic skirt and the rest of the dress over my head.

"Put your arms in!" she ordered me. "You have to help here!"

"I can't see!" I said. "I have a bag over my head!" All I could see was the huge zipper of the headdress in front of my eyes, but finally the dress was on and she and Judy fussed at me, zipping and pulling and buttoning.

"Can I take the bag off now?" I asked. "I feel like a POW." The woman didn't crack a smile as she handed me a pair of white high heels that just happened to be in the dressing room. My own shoes were still full of straight pins.

"You have to wear these," she ordered.

"But I have a bad knee," I whined, limping out to the three-way mirror in the main area of the shop.

"Just put them on so we can check the length of the dress," she said. I obediently did, seeing myself in the mirror in an enormous billowing white skirt and a fitted top that the clerk was still pinning with a vengeance behind me.

"Try this on with it," the owner of the shop came over and said, pulling a beautiful white shawl off the rack and handing it to the clerk. She gave the top one last pull before she put the shawl on my shoulders. "The skirt is made of shantung, but that shawl is silk. Dupioni silk, actually."

The only silk I was familiar with was soymilk, but I nodded in deference to all those silkworms who sacrificed their lives for fashion.

Meanwhile in the mirror, I looked like a drag queen. The clerk continued to fuss over me and I didn't want her to get into a worse mood, but I could feel my knee swelling up, and I knew I'd be toppling over soon, like a 6 story snow sculpture.

The next number was a cranberry one, and I had to wear the hood over the head again, and it turned out to be $1800. Kind of expensive for eight hours of my life. A few days later, after I'd finally escaped the hood tortures, we found the perfect dress at Norma Sharon's downtown— a plum colored sueded rayon—and that part of the wedding prep was done. Only four more months to go.

The week of the wedding came and all the plans were made, but since I'm older than the average bride, I thought I should get my face waxed three days before the big ceremony. I went to a Fancy Cheeks in town on a Wednesday evening. I told the technician my wedding was that Saturday and I wanted my face to be perfect for all the wedding pictures and so on.

The technician, who must have been seventeen years old if she was a day, put a mass of black tar on my face, and when she ripped it off, she gasped.

"Oh, no!" (You never want your face waxing technician to say that.) "Part of your chin came off; I mean, your skin. I mean, the skin on your chin. Really, it's just in two places," she reassured me. "It should heal in a week—ten days, tops!"

"I'm getting married in three days!" I shrieked. "I'm going to have two big brush burns on my chin?"

"I didn't know your skin was so sensitive," she said.

Then she treated me with oxygen, a different kind of oxygen than you get from just walking around, apparently. She told me to come back the next day and she'd put more oxygen on it. Then I went to see my makeup person, Jonathan.

"Oh, my God!" he said. "Were you in a car accident?"

"I got waxed," I explained. He pursed his lips and started to work on me, swearing under his breath.

"I would have sent you to a good technician," he said. "I hope I can fix this."

Somehow he did; even two nights later at the rehearsal party, you could barely tell. By the day of the wedding, my brush burns were almost gone. Maybe it was the oxygen. It also helped that Hector, my hair stylist, created a new hairdo for me with pink roses in it that complemented my plum colored dress, drawing attention away from my chin trauma.

Mark and I were married at Hyde Park Lodge and we only made one mistake. After we said our vows and exchanged rings, we walked out with ten minutes left to the ceremony and two songs still to be sung. The Maid of Honor and Best Man followed us, and then Jonathan and Hector ran along behind while the baffled harpist sang my favorite song, "Let it Be," without me in attendance. I barely had a chance to kiss Mark before Jonathan tapped me on the shoulder.

"I've got to check your lipstick," he said. "And let's put a little more foundation on your chin before the pictures." Hector fluffed my hair and I was ready for the public.

And now Mark and I have been married over seven years and, aside from our silverware being incompatible, we get along great. Luckily he does most of the cooking because I only know how to boil things. Actually, I can also bake in rare circumstances, and I'm pretty good at making smoothies in the blender. He suggested I do a TV show called, "Boiling with Terry" so we're working on that. My boiling technique is that I like to put things in water, turn on the fire, and then let them fend for themselves.

Anyway, Mark *likes* to cook. We're a perfect match cause I like to eat. And we take care of each other. We haven't gone contra dancing yet. I'm going to suggest we skip that.

5|21|15

10

HALF-NAKED SURFING

"I'm going to take up something really dangerous if I have to keep saying goodbye to you," I said as Mark waved to me from the doorway of the plane that would take him far, far away.

He didn't hear me, of course; he was preoccupied with getting a good space in the overhead luggage compartment. This was a few months after we'd met; he was taking a plane home to Baltimore where he lived, and I was going back home to Santa Fe on a later flight.

"Long distance relationships," I grumbled, alone now in Hawaii where we'd just spent a romantic nine days together celebrating my birthday. How come *he* never got emotional when we parted?

I sniffled my way out of the airport and drove off in the

rental car I had till midnight when my flight departed. What would I do with my last day in paradise?

I decided to visit Mark's younger brother, Ken, who lived on the north shore of Oahu. Haliewa was the town, a small hamlet with turquoise water surrounding it. Beautiful, I thought as I drove in, passing a sign that said, "Ice Cold Coconuts." I resolved to stop by there, later that day.

Sure enough, before an hour had passed, I was in the car with Ken and his girlfriend after shopping for health food for our dinner. My plan (since Mark and I hadn't gotten much sleep the night before) was to nap on the beach and call it a day. But first I had to get my ice-cold coconut. Ken agreed to stop and we pulled into the surf shop/coconut stand.

The first thing I saw was a tanned, handsome, thirty-something dude with a machete in one hand and a coconut in the other.

"This is Milton," Ken said.

Milton proceeded to chop off the top and I sucked the coconut juice through a straw. Then he chopped it in half and we all ate the coconut meat.

"How about a surfing lesson?" Milton asked me.

"Oh, I don't think so," I said. "I'm leaving Hawaii tonight and I'm pretty exhausted. Maybe next time."

"He's the best," Ken encouraged me. "He's surfed, like, 40 foot waves."

Impressive, I thought. Milton was smiling at me.

"But I've never surfed before," I protested. "I've never even used a boogie board."

Milton looked at me in my bathing suit.

"I can tell you're a natural," he said. "Even your stance." He put his hand on my arm. "It's destiny."

Always a sucker for flattery, I flexed my biceps and we agreed that I had the arms of a surfer.

The next thing I knew, I was on Ali'i, the beach where Baywatch is filmed, but David Hasselhoff was nowhere in sight. I noticed warning signs along the edge of the water.

"Should I worry about that strong current?" I asked Milton, who was lugging two surfboards under his arms.

"Nah," he said. "This was meant to happen today. You're right where you're supposed to be."

Where I was supposed to be, apparently, was the beach on a small inlet near the ocean, a peaceful patch of water with no waves where Milton proceeded to teach me the basics.

"Lie down on the sand where this line is," he told me. "Now pretend you're paddling." I did as instructed.

"Great!" he said. "Perfect!" He seemed a little too enthusiastic, if you asked me.

Next we entered the water and he showed me how to lie down on the surfboard.

"Now paddle in the water," he told me, "and when I tell you to, just pop right up and you'll be standing!"

It sounded easy, but I knew better. I felt clumsier by the minute as I tried the twist and pop up several times; my childhood memories of learning to tap dance and feeling completely awkward came rushing back to me.

"Maybe I need the remedial class," I said, falling off the

surfboard for the third time.

"No way!" Milton said, always cheerful. "You really have heart, you know that? Just going to buy a coconut and now you're surfing!" That made me feel better. "Besides, you know Jesus Christ was the first surfer, right? Cause he walked on the water."

"Wow, Sister Mercia never told us that," I said.

"Let's hit the ocean," Milton said. "You're ready."

I had my doubts, but off we went. I laid down on the surfboard and paddled toward the waves, Milton right behind me.

The first twenty minutes involved waves of all sizes pummeling me senseless. I achieved some spectacular wipeouts off my surfboard and I hadn't even caught a wave yet. I felt completely out of control as each huge wave crashed over me. I also consumed large quantities of salt water in this second stage of Surf-Hawaii.

"Surfing really is over-rated," I told Milton, but a wave covered my face before I could finish my sentence.

One of his directions earlier had been, "If you go under water, enjoy it. It's better than getting hit in the head with the surfboard." He had a point, but each time I slid off the board when a wave overtook me, I can't say I really enjoyed the green gurgling plunge into the deep. Though I didn't get hit in the head with the surfboard, so I wasn't able to evaluate that experience.

And finally I started to get better at holding on to the board even as countless waves washed over me. Progress, not perfection. Still, I barely had time to bask in my paltry power over the waves before Milton was next to me, ready to push me into Phase 3.

"Turn the board around!" he yelled since I was still headed out toward the ocean, my arms aching from all the paddling.

"I can't!" I yelled back. I kept using my free arm to paddle, but with the rough water, I couldn't turn the board so Milton got behind me and helped.

At long last, my wave came.

"Paddle!" Milton screamed. "Pop up!"

He pushed my board and I began to sail as the wave moved under me, carrying me.....I knelt on the board prepared to stand, but I was already being transported to the shore on my knees.

HOW CATHOLICS SURF, I thought. My mother would be proud.

Milton was behind me.

"Almost!" he said. "Next time, stand up!"

We paddled out again; this time I resolved to go all the way. My arms were aching, my nose was running, my hair was in my eyes, and the sky was turning shades of red and purple. The sun had gone down and I hadn't even noticed.

Finally a wave rolled in behind me and Milton guided me into it. I could feel its swell, lifting me up and then I was gliding....I stood up slower this time, not rushing it.

"Easy," I said out loud. "Easy does it," and then I was standing! I rode that wave victoriously, gloriously into shore.

Standing on water like Jesus. But when my board hit the sand, I realized I was unlike Jesus in one important way: my breasts had completely escaped from the top of my bathing suit.

I struggled to get my suit back on as waves pounded me and Milton approached.

"My suit is off!" I yelped to him.

"I know," he said. "As a teacher, I have to put up with this a lot." He grinned and gave me the high-five.

"You did it!" he said.

"Yeah," I said. "Let's do another one." We got back on our boards as darkness fell, and I realized I hadn't thought about Mark leaving all day. Surfing as therapy—it worked for me, especially when Milton was so chiseled. I felt a little guilty, but we paddled out to find the perfect wave again.

Next time, I'll ride that baby either with my suit all the way on, or all the way off. I hate to do things halfway.

11

WHY CAN'T THEY
LET US BE BEAUTIFUL?

"*If God sees to it that I get a second chance, I promise him and everyone else that I won't let them down. All I want to do is get out of here so I can start living my life again. I have a very wonderful life. I guess we don't see that until it's taken away from us. I have a beautiful daughter and a wonderful husband, the greatest man who by the way still loves me and believes in me. So, see, if I get my second chance, I'm going to stop feeling sorry for myself.*"

Every Friday afternoon, I visit with the women in the detention center on Airport Road, the Santa Fe County Jail. Most of the women, ranging in age from 18 to 55, are incarcerated for petty crimes like shoplifting, forgery, and stealing cars, though drugs are often involved. Many of the women are released after a few weeks or a few months from the county jail into society, though some are transferred to the prison in Grants to finish out their time.

"I feel like a baby. All I want is for my mom to love me, but she can't seem to forgive me for what I've done to her. I can't understand her; it's like she has no feelings. I feel so ashamed cause girls in here wish they had a mother, and me, I got one. But I wish I could talk to her; I wish I could be close to her like we once were not too long ago. I wish she would listen to me when I call her. I wish she wouldn't hang up the phone on me. I would tell her how grateful I am that she is bringing up my little girl. I can't believe what drugs have done to me. As I was growing up, I always wanted a baby. And now I can't even care for her because drugs took over my life."

I teach them creative writing. The guard always thanks me for coming but he still has to check me with the metal detector when I first walk in. Then we go to get the women. "Ladies! Creative writing!" he booms out, opening the steel door and they line up. "Left side, ladies! Left side against the wall!" he yells. Then we march to the library, a room with no windows. "How's the weather today?" the women always ask me.

"Locked up like an animal
Never to gaze at the stars
Or look at the sun..."

Before we begin, I open the bag of cookies, the container of chocolate kisses, and they munch as they listen to the story I read that I hope will get them to write. Sometimes they don't listen well; they whisper to each other or crane their necks to see out the library door where the men's unit is. Sometimes I get grouchy when they aren't listening, but I usually just read louder. "What's the topic?" they ask when I finish and I give them one I hope won't make them sad. "Could we just write about how we feel?" they ask. They put pen to paper, still opening foil-wrapped kisses and popping them in their mouths. I always write my story, feeling comfortable to say whatever I am feeling, even if I'm depressed or scared or angry. Whatever I write, they love. "You read first!" they always say, but I tell them to read theirs. Sometimes they cry when they read; sometimes they won't read at all, just hand me their piece and ask me to read it to myself later. I put it in my bag. I like reading my writing to them because they always clap; plus they relate when I'm upset, writing about a recent breakup. "You did right, girl, getting rid of him!" they tell me. "Another bad-ass man." Once I wrote that I wanted to go over and shoot him and one woman said, "Don't do that, girlfriend; you'll end up in here with us!" ●

One day while I read them a story, Margie started fixing Linda's hair. Linda had been wearing curlers, and she pulled them out as I was reading to them. As she sat there, Margie just quietly got up and began to fluff and comb Linda's hair with her fingers. It reminded me of the time I substitute taught in an inner city classroom in Los Angeles and was afraid initially because I didn't know the school or the neighborhood. But when I walked into the third grade classroom, one little girl said out loud, "Miss, you got purple hair!" From then on, we got along and at recess, the girls began to play with my curls as I sat on the playground swing, doing them up in Rasta braids. I loved having someone touch my hair, pulling it a little and smoothing it down. Later, those girls were wrestling with each other on the classroom floor, but I didn't yell at them much because I could still feel their sturdy brown fingers pulling my strands of hair—their fingers in my hair, making it strong.

I'm not sure why I visit the women in prison, except I thought if anyone needs to write, these women do. And I like the feeling of community. I've gone every week for seven years, and there are days when I don't want to leave when the time is up. After that breakup, for instance, when I felt like my emotions were leaking out all over, I craved a structure where I'd feel safe. Safe in jail, I know that sounds strange. Kind of like the safety I felt in my authoritarian family growing up. Not exactly enjoyable, but at least I knew I'd be in one piece in the morning.

The inmates help each other, though they don't always like each other. "That bitch," one says about the other behind her hand. Nevertheless, they stick together. They aren't allowed any makeup or perfume there, so they make their own, a batch of it for everyone. For lipstick, they use chapstick mixed with red ink; it also doubles for rouge. They smooth it on with their fingers. "Eyeliner" is simply applied with #2 pencils. Eyeshadow is made from cigarette ashes, and foundation is created from coffee grounds and hand cream. To make mascara, they mix black ink with toothpaste. They get hairspray at the commissary, but most of the women don't consider it strong enough. They add pancake syrup to the spray bottle so their hair will be stiff and styled. Nancy, a woman with deep track marks on her arms from a past heroin addiction, tells me how her cellmate got up in the middle of the night to do her hair. Twenty-five women in a room meant for fifteen, three women sleeping under the TV that's always blasting. "We only got one bathroom, so we gotta take turns," she explains. "We wait a lot."

"Life isn't easy here at all. I never want to come back over here, ever again. But why complain? Make the best of it while you're in here. Take it one day at a time. Be patient and wait."

I bring them "women's magazines" like Cosmopolitan, Vogue, Women's Day, Redbook, Glamour. Many of them have perfume ads inside, and the women rip them out and hide the pages in their green uniforms. "They don't let us have perfume here," they tell me. "We put it on letters to our men. Makes 'em crazy."

But one day when I came, the women seemed depressed.

"What's up?" I asked. "Don't you guys want to look at the magazines?"

Renee, one of the more outspoken women, tells me what happened. "They did a lockdown and strip search last week after writing class," she said. "Took not only our perfume ads but all our chapstick and red pen, toothpaste, mascara, everything. Why can't they let us be beautiful?"

The guard was listening. "What do you need makeup for anyway?" he asks. "All you see is each other. You don't go anywhere. You don't need makeup."

Linda stands up and looks at him. "We want to be beautiful for ourselves," she says.

The women deal with practical day-to-day matters. like getting out of jail. They ask me to edit a letter they wrote to a judge, a letter that hopefully will qualify them for a drug recovery program, rather than serve another year in jail. Some have parents or children who have been or were then incarcerated; many of the women are in for the third or fourth time. Jail is familiar to them, a cycle. Many have been victims of incest or other kinds of abuse. Elma, a nineteen year old woman who likes to write poetry, has cigarette burns on her arms, burns she inflicted on herself. "I don't know why I do it," she tells me, smiling shyly. Then she writes another poem.

> *Up on the hill of token dreams*
> *Down by the river of tattered streams*
> *Past the valley of misfit souls*
> *At the lake of the forgotten rose*
> *By the rapid snow blind sea*
> *And to the dark, damp, woeful tree*
> *Upon a frozen time*
> *Beside the book of rhyme*
> *I once loved*
> *Me.*

"Left side, ladies!" Once again the guard barks as we leave the library after our ninety-minute class. They search the women to make sure they don't return to their cells with any cookies, candy, or worst of all, perfume samples—though they hide them pretty well. Just before the door clangs shut, they thank me for coming. "See you next week!" they call out and I wave goodbye.

After Nancy attended for five months, she was moved to the Women's Prison in Grants and she writes me from there.

She has another year to serve on her drug possession charge.

"I have this faith. As you know, I have lots and lots of problems, but I try to see the good and positive side to all things. My thoughts and prayers are with you always."

These women are wounded as we all are, and they've made some mistakes. But they haven't given up. They've taught me about resilience and about forgiveness. Makeup or no makeup, these women are beautiful to me.

12

TRANSCENDENTAL HUGGING

7/22/14

"Hey, want to go see Ammachi?" my friend Jane asked in the parking lot after yoga class. I'd heard about this Hindu woman from India who was a spiritual leader. "She's really cool; I heard that seeing her can change your life."

This sounded good. I hadn't had a guru since Sister Theodora forced me to memorize 64 prepositions in fourth grade.

"You should really wear a dress though," my friend said, looking crosswise at the old blue jeans I was wearing. "Just out of respect cause Ammachi's like a saint."

Luckily I had a dress I was taking to the cleaners in the backseat of the car, so I changed in the bathroom and we were off, along winding Santa Fe roads to find nirvana.

Finally we arrived and it took forever to park because there were so many people, possibly thousands. We headed toward the tent and were told we couldn't enter it with our shoes on, so we placed them on a shelf along with a multitude of other tennis shoes, sandals, and Birkenstocks.

When we got inside, there actually were a few folding chairs left in spite of the crowd, but the ceremony had already started. I noticed many people had worn white: the women looking like priestesses in long, flowing gowns, and the men in tunic tops and linen pants, also in white like priests.

I never get the clothes right for these things, I thought. My dress was purple and bright and sleeveless, probably not modest enough to see someone holy. Plus my purple bra straps were showing.

Then Jane got up to talk to someone else she knew, so I ended up alone, desperately seeking spirituality from a short, plump, Indian woman I could barely see on the stage about a mile in front of me. The people on the stage were talking, one at a time into the microphone, some translating Amma's words into English for her. Then the whole audience began to sing and chant and Indian music was played. I felt mesmerized by it and closed my eyes, but that made me more aware that I was really starving. I hadn't eaten dinner, so I pulled my big black purse out from under my chair and searched for food. Emergency food—hadn't I thrown an oat bar in there recently? Apparently not; all I found was peppermint gum. I finally stopped rummaging, but the singing continued. I turned my head and saw a sign that said, "Indian food—$6 a plate will be served at 8:45

in kitchen tent," but I noticed the time was already 9:15. That was the problem with spiritual events; they needed a time management consultant. Wasn't anyone else starving? Or were they just going to chant all night?

"Did you get a ticket?" the older woman next to me asked.

"They're showing a movie?"

"It's for the hugs," the woman said. "Ammachi gives hugs that really can turn your life around."

"Wow," I said. I looked up at the stage and saw people lighting candles in front of her, seemingly praying to her.

"Are they worshipping her?" I asked the woman, who seemed to know what she was talking about.

"Not exactly," she said. "But Amma is the incarnation of the Divine Mother, like the Goddess presence in the universe."

"Like the BVM," I said. I'd always been a fan of the Blessed Virgin Mary, especially her outfits. She looked a lot better than I had in my blue prom gown.

"Go over to that table and you can get a ticket," the woman said. I walked over and stood in front of a young woman with a roll of tickets in her hand. I explained that I wanted to get a hug and the woman handed me a blue ticket with the number 389 on it.

"Is this your first time seeing Ammachi?" she asked. When I nodded yes, I was handed a blue dot. "Paste that on your chest," the woman said. "There are 388 people that will be hugged ahead of you. The blue dot is just so Amma can see that you're new."

"Yikes," I said on my way back to my seat. I was never going to last the whole night. "Don't these people ever eat?" I asked the woman next to me.

"After everything else is over," she told me. "Want some of my trail mix?" She pulled a bag of nuts and raisins out of her pocket and I dug in, girding myself for the long haul.

But soon I needed a rest room and was directed to the Port-a-potties outside the tent. I nearly stepped on a huge stinkbug and wished I had my shoes. I also wondered if I'd ever see my car again. It was now dark and we were in the woods. When I got back, the chanting seemed to be winding down; it was almost 10 pm. A dark man with a beard and a yellow tunic got on the microphone to make an announcement.

"Ammachi will now be giving her blessings," he said. "Please line up according to your numbers; the first one hundred people can move towards the stage now. The others waiting may go shopping at the booths in the back. We appreciate exact change."

Jeez, I thought. *Hare Krishna meets the Shopping Channel.* I looked around and drop cloths had been pulled off the tables in the back of the room; before me were all sorts of products from bubble bath to sandalwood jewelry. I headed to the rear tables where I sniffed soap, tried on beads, and perused books about Amma. There also were tee shirts and small statues of Indian goddesses and pictures of Amma. They seemed expensive, but it was better than that huge replica of the Sacred Heart with the bloody spear through it that my family displayed in every room when I was growing up. No wonder I still have trouble relaxing.

I saw my friend Jane again in the shopping area and she showed me her purchase: a string of sandalwood prayer beads. We agreed to stand in line together as soon as the sign went up for huggees between 300 and 400. But only those who had numbers up to 200 were being hugged then, so we went to the next tent and got in line for Indian food. They served cauliflower and carrots, jasmine rice, and dhal lentil soup—and it tasted a lot better than the food I cooked for myself.

Finally it was time for us to stand in line for our hug. We'd gotten to the center a little after 7:30 pm.; it was now 11:30!

One of Amma's disciples stood at the microphone again. "My brothers and sisters!" he said. "Some of you have been blessed by the Mother and are leaving. But be careful! There is no camping here. Remember, we are in the forest. There are bears and wildcats in these mountains. Be careful when you go to your car."

Maybe it was good that I was number 389; the bears would already have eaten by the time I tried to find my Toyota.

Jane and I sat on the floor as the line moved slowly to the front. Each time it crept even a foot, we had to get up, move a pace forward, and then sit down again. It was very good exercise, like squat thrusts in gym class. The other option was to kneel in line, then move forward on our knees, but then I'd probably need ten more years of therapy.

I watched the stage, noticing that one woman in a white sarong with a veil on her head carried what looked like a teddy bear that was also dressed in a sarong. The teddy bear even wore a turban!

That woman must be really devoted, I thought. Or nuts.

But most of the people on stage seemed sincere. People were lined up in front of Amma, and her assistants would nudge a devotee forward when it was time for his or her blessing. I tried to see Amma's face each time she hugged someone, but there were too many people in front of me. She sure had to hug a lot of people. I glanced at a program for the evening that lay on the floor near me; it explained how many charities Amma had in her name. I hadn't realized she helped the homeless, the sick, the orphans.

And it touched me that over and over, grown men and women were held in Amma's arms as if they were her own offspring held to her chest. If only the rest of the world was that open to giving and receiving love! I remembered how earlier in the evening when Amma had addressed the audience, her greeting was translated as she smiled out at everyone. "My precious children," she had said.

Then it was almost my turn and I was kneeling on stage with the others but I was told by one disciple who held a box of Kleenex that I should wipe my face. What's wrong with my face? I thought. Is it dirty? But I couldn't ask him since no one but Amma seemed to be talking then, and only in her own language. The man motioned for me to give him my glasses, so I did. I patted my face with the tissue.

"More!" the man whispered. I patted it a little harder, not understanding till much later that he wanted me to wipe off my Painted Desert lipstick. Then I was next to hug Ammachi, the embodiment of the Divine Mother.

I knelt down but was pushed from behind into Amma's chest. Amma turned my head, possibly so she wouldn't get a big lipstick kiss on her white gown, but it all went much too fast. I wanted to say, *"Help! I've always needed a mother to listen to me! I'm from an alcoholic family!"* But then I heard Amma's voice in my ear and it seemed to be saying, "No, no, no, no." I didn't know what I was doing wrong! Within moments, the attendants pulled me away and that was it, except for the Hershey's kiss and the rose petal that was pressed into my hand.

I sat down on the floor again with Jane, but then I realized Jane had a smear of holy white paint on her forehead.

"I didn't get anything on my forehead," I said. "I bet she didn't like me. She kept saying 'No, no, no.' The Divine Mother always liked you better."

We both watched the stage for a few minutes afterwards. A little girl of ten or so was in front of Amma, next to be hugged, but she was crying, her shoulders shaking. Amma saw her and pulled her to her chest for a long hug, then rubbed her back and talked to her. Then she motioned for the girl to come up on the platform with her and sit down!

"I should have cried up there," I said.

"I know," Jane said. "Plus that little girl got her back rubbed, too, the bitch!"

We decided to go back to the shopping area again, and were surprised to see a booth with dolls that looked exactly like Ammachi.

"Unbelievable," Jane said, picking one up. "Even this tiny doll is $45. And these bigger ones are $180!" I realized that the teddy bear with the white turban must not have been a teddy bear at all, but an Ammachi doll. Yikes.

We decided to ask the helper at that booth what Ammachi might have whispered in my ear.

"She kept telling me 'no,'" I told the helper. "She hates me!" I still felt unsettled that the hug hadn't been longer after four hours of waiting and that maybe I'd screwed it up somehow.

"I don't think she was saying 'no,'" the clerk told us. "Usually with women, she whispers 'daughter' in your ear. But with her accent and the way she repeats it, the sound is, 'do-ter, do-ter, doter.'"

Then I realized the hug had been sweet like the chocolate, just a bit short. My mother never had whispered "daughter" in my ear. I also remembered that Amma had shaken me in a playful way and seemed to be chuckling, though she could have just been shuddering when she saw my lipstick. But maybe the hug was exactly as it should have been. After all, the poor woman did have to hug at least five hundred people, twice a day.

I finally was ready to drive home after midnight, and I didn't get eaten by a mountain lion or bear on the walk to my car. In fact, I drove home singing "Somewhere Over the Rainbow" and felt as peaceful as the moon rising in the sky.

❖ ❖ ❖

13

SLEEP DEPRIVATION

4/22/14

My mother is 90 years old and she never wants to go to bed. No one in my family embraces sleep; we're all as hyper as Chihuahuas. I go to visit Mark's family, and they take naps on couches during family parties, but that behavior in my family is absolutely not allowed. If anyone falls asleep during one of our family get togethers, we take pictures, then turn the TV up really loud so they can see what they're doing is wrong.

My family's main goal is not to relax, but to entertain. When I was a kid, we used to stand in front of the refrigerator and do impersonations though I was really bad at them. But it tickled my father's funny bone, and that was the point.

Why does my family resist sleep so much? I don't know. When I was young and we threw family parties, my brother in law would show slides of our family projected onto our living room wallpaper, even though it had little pink shells on it which marched across a still shot of my sister Mary, poised to dive into a rich neighbor's pool, hands pointed at the water, her hair a Brillo pad of curls. Then talk would begin of how gigantic my brother Bob's head was, and later, once my brother Joe showed up at midnight when the party began at 8 pm, he'd say, "It's the shank of the evening!"

That was our cue to begin discussing how abnormally large Joe's left ear was. I remember still being up then at 4 am, eating the leftover Spanish peanuts from the clear plastic dish on the coffee table and laughing at my father, though I knew not to get too close once he had five beers.

Later, after he died, my brothers entertained me. They were always funnier than my sisters so I hung around with them.

As I've gotten older, I seem to go to bed later and later. Now that I'm married, and my husband is a morning person, he says goodnight about 11 pm., and I go in the bedroom and rub his back and we talk a little, but then I start singing a song to his butt.

"You are a child of the universe, no less than the trees and the stars, you have a right to be here."

"You have to go now," he says.

Maybe it's better that I go to bed much later because we both like to spread out in our King bed. Plus, before I go to sleep, I have to first exercise for 45 minutes on the elliptical machine in the garage. Then I have to finish my email, give my elderly cat her medicine, and take my 14 vitamins. My next step is to water all the household plants. Then I do Chigong, a series of Chinese movements, before it's time to wash up. When I'm finally ready for bed, I turn on the air cleaner in the bedroom to ease my allergies, put the fan on if it's summer, and then I place the Tropical Hurricane CD in my tape player. I put a cough drop in my mouth, a heating pad under my back because I have a pinched nerve, and I place my own pillows along both sides of my body, so if I roll over either way, my knees will have support.

"You're in my territory!" sometimes my husband will grumble, the boundary being the middle of the bed. Or else he just tosses and turns once I get in, and that's a signal that I'm disturbing him. Though he might have restless leg syndrome.

"It's too noisy in here!" sometimes he says. "How many machines have to be on?"

That's why sometimes I go to bed at dawn, right when he's getting up. I rarely get enough sleep, but I seem to be very productive in the middle of the night: doing laundry, washing my hair, grading student essays, writing. I feel calmer when it's dark outdoors and I don't have to make anyone laugh.

Once Mark finishes showering, if I'm still up, we talk and kiss for awhile, and watch the sun rise. Then we let our younger and fatter cat out, keeping an eye out for coyotes, and he says, "Since you're still up, want to go for a morning walk with me?"

I usually say no because I have to get some sleep before I teach my classes in the late afternoon and evening. So I put on my pajamas and burrow under the blankets and make sure the blackout curtains don't let any light into the bedroom. Then I put on my two eye masks, one over the other, stick in my purple earplugs, and settle in for a good day of sleep. Sometimes I get back up to turn on the humidifier.

I'm becoming the Saint of Sleep Deprivation.

❖ ❖ ❖

14

DON'T I KNOW YOU
FROM WAY BACK?

7/23/14

About seven years ago, when I was 50, I phoned my then 84-year-old mother in Buffalo to wish her a happy Valentine's Day. She was pleased I'd called, and we had a nice conversation. I was aware that she hadn't yet gotten around to her daily job of getting me back to the Catholic Church. Most of our conversations ended with her saying, "I want you to surprise me and tell me you're a good little Catholic again. Will you do that for your poor old mother?"

But today was different. She seemed cheerful and laughed at my jokes. She told me that the weather was better, the sun was out, and it hadn't snowed in a week or so. I suggested she go outside and take a little walk when my brother, who was bringing her dinner, came over.

"I'll wait till you come and visit," she joked.

"Then we'll go jogging," I kidded. "And by the way, I sent you some chocolate for Valentine's Day; you should get it in a day or so."

"Oh, good, I love chocolate," she said. "I'll be looking for it."

"Well, I might have forgotten to put my name on the card," I told her. "I was at the post office yesterday, but I was in a hurry . . ."

"What name would you have put on the card?" she asked, laughter in her voice. "Who is this?"

"It's Terry, Mom."

"And where do you live?"

"In Santa Fe, Mom, remember? For the last nine years." She often asked me where I lived but had never forgotten my name before.

"And what's your last name?" she asked.

"Wilson, Mom. Same as yours."

"Oh, yeah," she said. "Your voice sounds familiar. Don't I know you from way back?"

I felt like someone had just punched me in the stomach. She had forgotten me. Her mind, like a faulty computer, could not process who I was anymore. I knew her mind had been slipping some in the past few years: she'd been repeating herself and occasionally forgetting how many children she had. But I was still in denial — how could this have happened to my mother? She was the one in our family who had always held everything together. Having buried two husbands, she was the one who had handled the money for our family, who had taken us to buy our Easter clothes, who had taught me to drive.

The following week I attended an Alzheimer's group in downtown Santa Fe for the first time. And when I explained that my mother didn't know me anymore, I cried. But there were stories much worse than mine. One man told how his wife had gotten Alzheimer's when she was 50, and now she could say only four words. He'd had to lock up the Drano or else she'd drink it. Another man talked about how his father moves large rocks to the corner of the backyard, then moves them back again. "He keeps busy," he said, trying to joke about it.

But no one could change what had happened — my mother becoming a stranger. I have five brothers and sisters who, along with the women we pay to take care of my mother, help her stay in her own home instead of going to a nursing facility. Still, each time I went to visit her, she continued to decline. She lost her front teeth to decay — my fussy mother whose first question whenever I changed jobs was, "What kind of dental plan will you be getting?" She wandered out in the street one cold December night at 4 a.m.; fortunately, a police officer found her and took her home and called my brother. She's still at home but has needed full-time care ever since.

I see my mother disappearing now, becoming more fragile by the day. I hate the thought of her being gone, ever. But that good-looking, fastidious, bossy mother whom I grew up with has disappeared . . . OK, she's still bossy. These days we've all adapted to the fact that my mother is the center of attention, which she never used to be because as a Catholic woman she came last. She only took one fish stick for herself, and she served herself last. Today, though, if it's her birthday, nothing is predictable because she puts my gift of a sweater on her head and she makes faces when anyone in the family reads her their sentimental "I love you, Mother" cards. Sometimes she falls over on the couch as if she's been shot or she sticks out her tongue. Lately she's been rolling her eyes and saying in a falsetto voice, "Lovely!" She's become a supreme entertainer.

Which brings me to the question: is Alzheimer's all bad? It feels pretty awful a lot of the time because of the erosion of abilities and of recognition: of family, of one's own skills. But what about the good side—that we learn intimacy by dealing with this person, that maybe she wasn't so happy being in control of everything and now she just lives day to day? I suppose I want to think that something about it is good or I'll go insane, seeing my mother so different from the competent person she used to be.

Luckily, my family is expert at dark humor. We all see the tragedy, but we still can laugh at the funny parts. I may think it's rude that my older brother says that my mother now looks like a "bad pumpkin," but that's him trying to cope with the unthinkable: that the mother whom he loved for so many years — even if grumpy in her old age — is now this mother who takes little pieces of bologna from her sandwich and puts them in her jewelry box to save them. It's hard to get your mind around these insane and heart-wrenching changes, so you cope however you can. We now try to live with the sorrow of our own mother losing her mind. But we still want to see her, hug her, take care of her, bring her bananas, cookies and fudge — things she continues to like.

As I write this, I notice the amaryllis in my office with two tall stalks: the drooping one has dead flowers on it, and they crumble if you touch them. Then there's that other stalk standing straight up, with its huge bright red blossoms. It's gaudy and bold, and somehow I think those flowers will never wilt — they'll never look like the other stalk — but then in a few days, they'll be as dead as the others and I'll somehow accept that. Yet even when I throw away dead plants — put them in Hefty bags and twist a tie around the top — it's hard to put them into the trash barrel. I can almost hear them screaming from inside the plastic bag, "Give me another chance! Don't give up on me!" Once I actually spared a few of my dead plants from the garbage truck and put them on my cement stoop out back. The next thing I knew, two of the plants had begun growing leaves again — they'd resurrected! When you're raised Catholic, you always think things have another life once they push the stone away from the tomb and rise up to greet the sky again.

Will my mother ever rise up again? I give money to the Alzheimer's Disease Research Foundation, so, yes, I hope that even though my mother is 90, she'll be able to benefit from a new drug that can bring some of her mind back. But not the worrying part, the anxious part — the part that 20 minutes after she got to any family gathering led her to say, "When are we going home? Enough is enough."

She still says, "I want to go home," but usually she's already home when she says it. Now we understand that "home" means that either she wants to use the bathroom or she wants to get into her bed, where she feels in control, smoothing the sheets and blankets around her and lifting them only to the middle of her chest — no higher or she gets cranky. And her door has to be half-open — not three-quarters open or a sliver open — but half-open so she can see out and keep tabs on what's happening in the house.   ♪

Sometimes she gets up in the middle of the night and picks up her purse, telling the woman who watches her at night, "I'm going to church now." The woman says, "No, Dorothy, you're in your pajamas. It's very cold out and it's 2:30 in the morning. Go back to bed." And my mother says OK and goes back to her bedroom, puts her purse on her dresser, lies down and then smoothes her covers under her hands once again.

Maybe some baby boomers are more Zen about dying than I am. Maybe some say, "When it's my time, I'll go peacefully" or "I don't want to live if I don't have my wits about me." But would I rather have had my mother die 10 years ago when she just began forgetting things? Would I rather have missed her holding my hand even if she couldn't remember my name, saying, "You're my darling girl"? She never once said that to me when I was growing up! Would I have wanted to miss how she laughs when I dance with her or when we sing old songs like "Way Down Upon the Suwannee River"? Would I prefer that she had left this Earth sooner? No.

I admit that it's hard to be around her sometimes, to see how hollow her cheeks have gotten, just like her mother's before her. And I hate that she sometimes makes a mess in the bathroom and has to be cleaned up. Or that the women who take care of her have to force her to take a bath every other day, she who always took such pride in her appearance. Some people say that you should be careful about who you turn out to be because every unresolved issue you're still angry about comes back magnified when you get old or get dementia. Still, my mother's caretakers love her. They pray with her, watch TV with her, eat with her, make her laugh.

Getting old is rarely simple. How do we age gracefully? And how do we accept another's aging process when it feels so out of our control? One important lesson I've learned is to listen to what the aging person needs. Last November, when I visited my mother, she gave me a glimpse into what it's like to be elderly and not in charge of her life anymore.

It was a Sunday afternoon in November, and I was trying to get her dressed for the day. The rest of my family was at the Buffalo Bills' football game. My mother and I had just spent an hour sitting on the couch watching Lawrence Welk on TV. We sang along to old favorites like "Me and My Shadow," a song my parents used to dance to. But now it was time to get my mother's pajamas off and her slacks and sweater on — she's chronically cold, even though her home thermostat is set at 80 degrees in the winter.

"Come on, Mom," I said, mostly because it's important to my older sister that my mother not wear her pajamas all day. "Let's put on a clean sweater and pants, and you'll look so nice when everyone gets back!"

Suddenly, she stood up, grabbed my shoulders with a

surprisingly strong grip, and turned me around. "Push, pull!" she shouted. "Push, pull! Now I'll fix you! See how you like it!" Then she laughed and laughed, and I gave up trying to get her pajamas off — she wore them under her clothes that day. And I realized what was really important: for my mother to be warm and comfortable in her own home and for her to feel like she had some control over something. My mother taught me a lot that day.

I wouldn't wish Alzheimer's on anyone. But it does create the possibility that we'll learn more about loving the person who has it, and we might even be able to forgive any problems that have come before in our relationship. It also can guarantee that we will have to deal with our own mortality while caring for the loved one who is saying the long good-bye.

Three months ago my mother fainted. She was taken to the hospital, and it turned out that her potassium had been low. After she woke up, the doctor asked her what her name and address were — he wanted to find out if she was oriented to her surroundings. She answered those questions correctly. Then he stated his last question.

"Do you know where you are?"

"Of course I know where I am," my mother responded.

"Well, then, where are you?" the doctor asked.

"I'm right here," my mother snapped.

Alzheimer's is teaching my mother to be "right here." And I'm learning to be "right here" along with her because I know these moments are all we have, precious moments that teach me how to live today and love her with everything I am.

❖ ❖ ❖

15

WHITE YARN

Inside my kitchen cabinet, there hides a box of millet and oat flake cereal, but the box is almost empty. The reason I keep it (and even moved it from my last house) is because inside is a cup of stale cereal in a plastic bag that has a piece of white yarn tied around it. Here is its story.

One time about eleven years ago, I went to visit my mother in Buffalo; she was 80 years old then. She'd just gotten out of the hospital after getting a hernia in her intestine repaired. My mother never got sick, never went to hospitals, never took any medicine, but one day when my sister Mary, the nurse, went over there, my mother said she couldn't keep anything down. She'd been throwing up for a few hours and when my sister asked what was wrong, she lifted her shirt and there on her abdomen was a big lump.

"Mom, why didn't you tell me this was happening? We need to go right to the hospital!"

"I'm fine," my mother said.

"But you have a huge bump..."

"It's only the size of an orange," my mother said. "We should at least wait till it's the size of a grapefruit."

"Let's go, Mom," my sister said, and they were off.

When they got to the hospital, the doctors could not believe that my mother's only medication was a half an aspirin a day. She was soon knocked out with the anesthesia and came through the surgery just fine.

Now I was visiting her at home, ten days later. She still moved a bit slowly, but in general she was much better. Though the anesthesia had affected her thought processes.

"Mom, do you want me to vacuum for you?" I asked her. I was about to stay in her guest bedroom.

"Oh, Jack and I vacuum all the time," she said. Jack was my then 87 year old stepfather who was on oxygen and also used a walker because without it, he'd fall over. I didn't think he'd been doing much vacuuming lately. I vowed to clean up my mother's house when I could get away with it, maybe while she was at church. Except I might have to be the one to take her there, since my stepfather could no longer drive.

"The house looks fine," my mother said. I agreed with her because she seemed grumpy. She got even more grouchy as the week went on because one morning at breakfast, Jack began to yell at her. She'd just finished nagging him about doing his leg exercises.

"I'm not the sick one; you are!" he said. "You just got out of the hospital and you won't rest. You could have died! If Mary hadn't forced you to go to the ER..."

"Oh, dry up," my mother said. "I'm OK now, aren't I?"

They seemed to argue a lot while I was there, and I felt pretty useless till one night Jack came into the living room in his pajamas and said to us, "Can you help me? That boil on my back broke again." He lifted up his pajama top and there was the most disgusting bloody hole in his back. "Just wash it and put a band aid on it," he told me. My mother was still mad at him for yelling at her two days before, so I had to do the dirty work.

The week went very slowly, and my mother wouldn't let me help her with anything, even taking the ten steps down into the basement to do laundry, though the doctor had forbidden her to. If I tried to do her laundry while she slept, she woke right up and yelled from her twin bed: "What're you doing out there? Get the hell into bed! I can't sleep with you gallivanting around!"

I tried to take walks, but one day Jack grabbed my arm and said, "It's dangerous around here. You can't just be wandering around the neighborhood."

"Jack, we're in the suburbs. People are out cutting their lawns, there are kids on swings...."

"Doesn't matter," he said. "A girl was found dead the other day."

"Where?" I said.

"I don't know. I think it was close to here."

I ignored them and took walks anyway, but sometimes

my mother would yell at me when I returned. "You were gone hours!" she'd say.

"Mom, I was gone forty five minutes," I'd correct her.

"Why can't you just walk up and down the driveway?" she'd ask.

One day I tried to get away from them and sat on the back porch, but my stepfather came in and began to tell me about this stump in the backyard that he'd tried everything to get rid of. "First, I tried chopping it down," he said. "No luck. Then I put some chemical on it—supposed to kill it but no dice. Finally I just got some dynamite and blew the thing up."

"That's great, Jack," I said.

It turned out that the whole week I stayed at my mother's, my brothers and sisters had cottages at the lake. I wanted to join them and swim but my mother wouldn't let me use her old car. I had three days left of vacation before I had to go back to work.

"Mom, you're not even using the car," I said.

"You never know when I need to fly somewhere," she said.

"But Mom, I just want to go swimming!" I told her. "I need a little vacation!"

"Well, I need a vacation too!" she said. At first I didn't know what she meant because she hadn't worked in years, but then I realized she needed a vacation from herself.

Finally my brother in law called to say he'd come into town and pick me up. My brothers and sisters didn't mind leaving me with my mother and stepfather because they thought I needed to suffer, to pay for living out of town and not having to take care of my mother and stepdad. But my brother in law took mercy on me.

"Marty is taking me out to the lake, just for today and I'll come back in the morning, OK?" I said.

"Oh, all right," she said. "What are you going to eat while you're there?"

"I think they'll have provisions, Mom. But I'll bring some of my health food, too."

I filled up a couple plastic bags with my bathing suit, a towel, and my oat bars and millet cereal that I put soymilk on. Then I waited by the door for Marty to show up.

My mother inspected the bags. "You didn't pack this well enough," she said, looking inside my already opened cereal box.

"It's fine, Mom," I said.

"No, I need to fix it," she said. She rummaged in the dining room drawer (which no one had seen the bottom of for years) and pulled out a piece of white yarn. Then she proceeded to tie the yarn around the tip of the bag of cereal inside the box, and finished by closing its flip top. Just then Marty's car horn honked.

My mother kissed me on the cheek. "Have fun," she said. "Be careful. And don't forget to come back!"

I wish I could say the same thing to her now because her dementia has made it impossible for her to come back. But at least I have that little bag of cereal tied with white yarn to remind me that my mother once was able to take care of me. I can't bear to throw it away.

16

LEARNING TO PLAY
THE MARIMBA

7/23/14

It was summer, and I felt at loose ends. I'd just left my full time job and would still be teaching part time, but I felt like some of my identity had disappeared. I needed something to ground me.

One day I remembered how much I'd loved those golden bells that had been on the altar each time I went to Mass as a kid. How the altar boy had rung them and their chimes flooded the church. I could never touch those bells because girls couldn't be on the altar, but I've always loved African music, in particular, the mbira, steel prongs inside a gourd that sounded like a bell. Except I didn't want calluses on my fingers. I wanted the music to be fun, so I decided to join a marimba class.

The first time I went to the class, the maker of the marimbas didn't answer the doorbell where the class took place, though he owned the building. He was on the roof, making repairs, and when he saw Mark and me, he came down the ladder and told us that the class had been cancelled that week. With no shirt on and his hair in a ponytail, he showed us his studio where a row of wooden marimbas stood, waiting to be played. He taught us the first few chords of Skokiana, a beer drinking song from Zimbabwe. The notes did sound like bells, clear and resonant. I was thrilled, and we bought a soprano marimba that night.

When we came home with it, Mark stuck post-its naming all the notes on the marimba, and he began to teach me a little about music. I've never played an instrument before; my only claim to fame was two weeks of tap dancing lessons when I was seven. I learned "brush-brush, ball, step," and I think I liked it, but then my mother pulled me out because we ran out of money.

That next week I started the marimba class with a middle aged woman named Alberta and about six other women. I loved the sound, but I felt clumsy because all the other women had much more experience than I did. Alberta did teach me some patterns and chords of songs, but sometimes the other women in class tried to help me.

"Hold your mallets like this!" one woman named Nancy told me. "I'm a chiropractor and I know a lot about shoulder strain."

I knew she was right, but I was still trying to memorize the notes and hit them the right way and not mess up any of the songs they were playing. I held the mallets so tightly my neck hurt, but I couldn't concentrate on everything at once.

Then another woman tried to help me as the class was ending. I'd had a lesson with Alberta a few days before, and she taught me some chords to a song called "Siakadumisa," a hymn from Zimbabwe. I felt good that I knew at least a few chords now, but this woman, Diane, was showing me something different that day.

"No, no, you need to vary those chords," she said. "Come on, you can do this. It's not that hard. Like THIS." And she played a few different chords again and I was supposed to get it but by then, after 90 minutes of class, my brain couldn't take anymore in. I didn't want to learn variations on the chords I'd learned; I wanted to just keep the few chords that I knew and not get myself all mixed up.

"You all are so generous, helping Terry," Alberta said then. "What a great group of women you are!" I smiled, but I backed away slowly from Nancy, Diane, and even Alberta at that point, and resolved to practice when I got home.

But then I did learn "Siakadumisa," and I learned more chords to "Skokiana," and I was beginning to feel like I might actually be able to master this instrument.

Except after about six weeks in this class, Alberta emailed me that the class had decided to change the night they met.

"But I can't meet on Tuesday nights," I complained to my husband. "I teach that night."

Alberta told me about some other classes I could join, so

the next week, I took the plunge. An older woman named Suzanne had emailed me back about her class at Wild Woman Studios on Siringo Road, so I rang the doorbell of her studio one rainy Monday afternoon. ☙

"Hello!" she said, as welcoming as could be. "I hope you like kids!" Then the children began wandering in, and they started to play the marimba with no direction from her. More and more bounded in, all between the ages of 8 and 14.

Meanwhile, I stood in front of the marimba she'd pointed me towards, except I didn't know the song they were playing. She saw me standing there like a dope.

"Honey, do you know "Madness?" I shook my head. "It's easy," she said. "You just hit these keys," she showed me a chord and then another one. "Then you hit these....come on, you try it."

I needed the instruction to be slow and simple; I wasn't getting all of what she was teaching. I tried one chord and got it wrong. Meanwhile, two sets of parents of kids had walked in and watched us.

"No, like this!" she said, showing me again, then walked away.

"OK," she said, excited, to the group of kids and me, "let's try it again!" The kids began to pound on the marimbas, banging and wailing out as loud as their marimbas would play.

I hit a few tentative notes but they sounded wrong. I did get one of the chords, so I kept playing it at intervals. I couldn't even hear myself play, so I tried hitting my mallets harder. And harder. And faster. The kids were playing so fast, I felt like I had a sharp knife inserted over my left eyebrow. I thought "Madness" would never end. My only comfort was that one little girl of about 8 seemed as lost as I was. She was just hitting random notes every now and then. We caught each other's eye at one point and grimaced.

After the class, Suzanne came over to me.

"You did great!" she said. "You really "got" "Madness!"

"I did?" I said, but she had walked away and began to talk to the parents again, parents who had proudly watched their kids play. Good thing *my* mother was busy that day with dementia.

● I knew I needed to find another marimba class, so I decided to check out one more the next day at the First Christian Church near downtown. A guy named Paul was teaching it, and that first class went OK, though again, I was not even a third as skilled as the other students. I had to leave early for a therapy appointment, and I was relieved.

But I decided Paul was a good teacher, so I went back. He assigned me a tenor marimba, and that second class, I was trying to concentrate on the notes, as usual. Since the marimba in class did not have post-its on it, I could only try to memorize how the colors of the wood sometimes changed for a "C" or an "E," and the "F sharp" had lighter wood with a pattern on it.

● I was just barely keeping up, when I noticed two women wander in from outside and begin to dance in the aisle between the pews of the church. One woman with gray hair was kind of pretty in an older hippie-baggy pants-and tank top-with size A breasts-and leg hair sort of way. She was dancing around as if she thought she was very cool, just waving her arms or leaving them outstretched straight like she was flying, and then she gazed at heaven like Jesus, except she was moving her hips more. Then the next moment, she was bounding across the room or swaying meaningfully to the music, her white hair hanging then flying around as she twirled. The other woman was lying on the floor at the back of the church with only her feet showing. I realized I was glad the class was held in the First Christian Church because the acoustics are great, but the vibes felt weird because the pews reminded me of all the times I'd felt trapped in church, trying to pray enough to impress my mother.

Anyway, the woman lying on the floor with face up, eyes closed, shoes off and bare feet, looked like she was dead, but maybe the marimba music was inspiring her. All I knew was that the woman whirling around, her gray head whipping in the dead air was really DISTRACTING ME! I could see her wheeling out of the corner of my eye and then I'd miss a note. Paul the teacher would give me a dirty look, and I'd lose my place and not be able to find it again till a minute later in the song. I was paralyzed, my marimba mallets raised two inches above the notes, wondering if it was time to come in again. Then I'd try, and Paul would shake his head. Next, he'd slowly start again on the chords from his place at the baritone marimba and finally I'd recognize the beat again and come in, feeling retarded. And still, Miss Cool Older Hippie Marimba Dancer was bouncing around right in my line of vision so I'd lose a note again!

But by the end of the class, the two women had disappeared (or been murdered) and we began to play Siakadumisa.

One of the other students was singing the words, and best of all, I knew the chords to it, and the sound echoed off the wooden walls of the church, way up into the ceiling, the chimes of bells. I've been humming the song ever since, those holy bells vibrating in my bones.

17

I SUCK AT LETTING GO

Tonight I've gotten a little window into how sad the world can be. My 17 year old cat, Butch, is in the Emergency Animal Hospital for two days and she has some kidney failure and a bad urinary tract infection. I'm so sad about it that I can't concentrate, but I know it's not just about my cat. It's about how intractable loss is, how I'm no match for it. LOSS just mows everything down in its path like a huge weed-eater. It has no regard for who it affects, and how. All I can think about is my Butchie, lying in that cold hospital cage with a catheter in her patuti and an IV in her leg or wherever the hell a doctor would put an IV in a cat that weighs only 7 lbs. Poor little skinny Butch, lying on that cold steel table tonight when I left her; I couldn't help crying at the sight. Mostly I just feel so powerless, so completely without any power to act....so hard for me. I know I'm bad at acceptance; I feel so paralyzed tonight that I can't seem to make myself do anything. It's like I'm in a trance. Maybe I should call the Prayer People, Silent Unity, though they might say it's stupid to pay $600 for a 17 yr. old cat to fix a urinary tract infection when so many people are suffering and Save the Children on TV is asking people to donate $22 per month to change a kid's life. I see how willing I am to save my little cat, no matter how much it costs. I also see how I want to blame my husband Mark for this, but he SHOULD have had the blood tests done on Butch when he took her in— he was trying to save money! But the truth is, I could have taken Butch to the vet myself that time....I was working and tired and didn't want to get up early on my weekend.

Of course I want to blame someone because pain and loss is so hard to accept! Goddamn it! Who among us has learned how to accept loss? If I was a Buddhist....well, I guess I'm not enough of one. How would Buddhists deal with this? Would they say, "Well, she's lived a good life, she's 17 yrs. old, let her go." But why should I be willing to let my little friend go if I can save her? I'm going to try to do everything I can to keep her alive unless she's in pain. The doctor said she's not. And isn't the urinary tract infection curable? With antibiotics— but I'm going to have a lot of trouble giving them to her on my own! If she doesn't drink enough or pee enough or take her antibiotics, she'll die. I'm mad at you, God!

And why shouldn't I be sad about my little girl? I remember the time she climbed up into the birdhouse and stuck her head out and that was so funny. And she used to greet my car each day when I came home...and she slept with me, cuddled under my knee.....and she ran to the phone when I called (when I was out of town), attracted to the sound of my voice. And she always had a shoe fetish. She loved to nuzzle my sandals and all shoes, to massage the sides of her face. And she loved to be in the bathroom with me because I was a captive audience and I'd pet her then. And when I was in the bathtub, she jumped up on the side of the tub and would meow loudly when I sang, even though I thought I sounded pretty good. She hated when I sang, but that made me laugh. ●

She's always been a one woman cat; she's never warmed up to anyone but me. She lies next to me while I do my back exercises, and she cuddles with me. She still always joins me in the bathroom and scratches to get in the door when I close it without letting her in. She still climbs in and out of the empty tub when I'm on the toilet, even with her arthritis, though this week she was more sluggish and now I know why; the poor thing was sick.

And I feel guilty that sometimes we've paid more attention to my other cat, Sylvester because he's more charming at times and it's harder to love an old cat because they're more idiosyncratic and not quite as clean or lively....Butchie, I'm so sorry if I've ever been grumpy with you or not been as loving as I could be....but I adore you and I want you to pull through this, OK? Please? Will you stick around longer?

There are just no guarantees in life and it sucks. But God, if you're there, could you let Butch live another several years? And my mother too, but also help us find the money to pay for her care? And Mark, of course, Mark, I want him to live forever. And I want to live forever too. I can't help it! How does one learn to accept loss if one has never been good at it? I somehow accepted the loss of my father, but did I? Time helped. But it definitely felt like a knife in my side whose pain gradually lessened, but will never be gone. And too bad if anyone thinks I should not be so upset about a little cat! I am, goddamn it!

I don't know how to let go of this even enough to go to bed tonight! But I have to; I have to call the vet when I wake up, and find out how she is, or at least visit her there, which could be heart breaking.

I wonder if I could just accept how I'm feeling tonight—angry, sad, full of grief, shock, sorrow, fear. And just let it be that way for now. That's what a Buddhist would do, maybe. I guess that's better than fighting all these feelings, but I sure want to resist them because I don't want the reality to be true, that Butch has kidney damage and that her prognosis at this point is not good. Right now, all I can accept is that I feel very sad and upset and a little angry and a lot fearful, but I'm still hoping that even though she's in the hospital now, she can still live a while longer with the right care. And I'm going with that, tonight, damn it!

Later that night I called Silent Unity, the prayer people. An older woman answered the phone.

"How may we pray with you this evening?" she asked.

I started to cry right away. "My little cat is in the hospital," I sobbed.

"I'm sorry, dear. What's the cat's name?" she asked.

"Butch," I said. "And my mother is sick too, because she's almost 90, and the cat reminds me of her because...."

"What did you say the cat's name was? We didn't quite hear you."

"Butch," I said again, wondering who else was listening in on the call.

She started to pray, "Lord, we affirm that Butch is healed and that all his cells will feel God's healing light..."

"Butch is a SHE," I said.

"A female cat named Butch?"

"Yes, she has a goatee, but she's female. And she's always acted a little tough, so I named her "Butch."

"I see," said the old woman.

"She's not really gay, she's just feisty," I said. "Not that I wouldn't love her if she was gay."

"Your mother is gay?"

"No, she's just feisty. So is Butch. Neither one is really gay. That I know of."

"Let's get on with the praying," she said.

One evening, about eight months after this, I was trying to meditate in my office at home, lying on the old tan rug. I thought maybe I could lie still because I wasn't just meditating, I was accomplishing something else. On that particular evening, I lay there with my traction device pulling my neck out away from my head, a contraption I'd gotten from a physical therapist because I have a herniated disk in my neck. The small steel grips dug into my scalp, and I tried to find a comfortable position on the floor and then closed my eyes. I took a deep breath. If I could drift off, I could ultimately make my neck feel better, plus contemplate at the same time.

Suddenly I felt the pressure of small paws climb onto my chest. I opened my eyes to see Butch, looking right into my eyes. She carefully positioned her skinny body right below my neck and continued to stare at me. I knew she was possibly dying, and the vet could not do much for her ailing kidneys anymore. I began to cry. I lay there, sniffling, but she gazed at me calmly. I don't know what cats think, and I don't know if she meant to communicate with me that day. But I felt her saying, "Don't worry; it's OK. You're going to be fine. Even if I die, I'm still here with you, right above your heart."

❖ ❖ ❖

18

SAILING AWAY

I loved to read fairy tales when I was a child as I sat in the old blue armchair at the edge of the living room. I felt I had no story, no real life, nowhere to go, no one to hold on to who knew me or who mattered. I lived with Bluebeard and princesses and ships and I floated away on my own boat; I sailed wherever I wanted and I became that princess who let her hair down so the prince could climb up its golden weave and save her. Those stories convinced me that miracles could happen, that pain could be transformed, that I could survive. I loved to dive into Laura Ingalls Wilder and the Beany Malone books about family and how happy they all were around the fire, sharing the one orange they got for Christmas, grateful for the cozy company as the snowy wind whirled outside their pioneer house, grateful for each other. I didn't feel grateful for my family—I knew I should just like all the other things good girls should do, but sitting in that chair I didn't have to be grateful, I didn't even have to be in that family anymore, until they called me for dinner two or three times and I finally heard them.

I loved the idea of sailing away, that idea of freedom. Occasionally I let my sister Ann come with me; we'd sit on the couch and pretend it was a boat. I was always the captain; she was a lowly sailor, swabbing the deck with a mop. But I was in charge of navigation; I organized our supplies: Ritz crackers, doll clothes, two bananas and all our underwear—everything we needed for survival. I steered the boat to wherever it was we were going —or maybe we were going nowhere—the destination seemed much less important than the fact that I was out there alone and free with no one telling me what to do or who to be. Only the sun was my company since I usually left Ann behind and just voyaged in the blue chair with the same number of supplies—who needed a deck hand anyway when I had the blasting sun and the salty waves and the rocking of my boat? And the fire in my heart that told me I was brave and true.

I liked the idea in the books that girls could sleep and be lovely while some handsome prince kissed their red lips and made them breathe again. I saw this not as dependent but as miraculous. Or maybe being beautiful and loved seemed like enough. I didn't see the trap that in order to be saved, I had to wait for the savior—the opposite of being free. But Jesus hung on the cross and he got redeemed by himself—with only a little anguish—just 40 days and 40 nights thirsting in the desert, and a few nails right through his skin and bone, and then thorns piercing his scalp and a sword cutting open his heart. And so I learned suffering could redeem, but I wasn't that interested. Not in that much agony—and besides, even if a woman suffered, could she redeem the world? Or even the turkey in the oven? My mother ached continually—at least that was what her face said—but she never got redeemed.

Purposefully sailing away, my hand on the steering wheel seemed like my best bet. Floating away from all the suffering; the nails; the blood; the turkey; my father, the savior for whom I had waited, but he was taking too long—drinking beer after beer in the living room and watching the Buffalo Bills. I wished he could make me whole again but he was busy.

I don't think I ever admitted to anyone that I took all those voyages because I knew I was supposed to be emulating my mother and waiting for my father to remember he had a daughter. I would've let my father go with me and I would've even let him steer the boat. I knew he had that same ruddy complexion I had from watching the sun go down and feeling the salt air wash our faces with mist—but he drank that beer and forgot everything except where the can opener was, so I had to go alone. And I did, I kept that sailor dream alive while I voyaged to freedom. I couldn't have even said it but I was sailing through the twisty hurricane to that big, blazing, wild sun: to myself.

19

MINDFULNESS

"Try to stay in the present," my therapist said to me. I've been in therapy for years; in fact, I've retired five therapists before this one. But my current therapist hadn't given up on me yet. She and I had been discussing how, even if I wasn't good at meditating, I could still practice using my workouts as a meditation.

"Swimming could work as a mindfulness exercise," she said. "Just try to notice what's happening as you swim. Slow down the movement of your arms, your legs; be aware of how they slip through the water and what color the water is and the sky."

This sounded good since I earned my Pollywog badge when I was six, but I mostly don't swim indoors because the chlorine is too hard on my skin and hair. Luckily, though, it was still summer and there are a few bodies of water around Santa Fe. That weekend, I talked my husband into going with me to Heron Lake, about a two hour drive north. Since it was the end of August I was hoping the water would not be too cold, but as we got closer to our destination— near the Rocky Mountains— the temperature was hovering in the 60's. &

I was determined to swim though; I'm a little obsessive about exercising every day. Once we arrived at the lake, I sat in the open car door with my feet on the ground and squeezed myself into my rubber wetsuit. My husband zipped up the back for me, and we walked on the rocks down to the water.

I got in slowly, but damn, it was COLD! I kicked my legs and splashed with my arms as hard as I could to warm up, but it still felt like I was in the icebox. I had asked Mark to time me so I could get a good workout. But then I wasn't mindful of anything but how long I had been in.

"HOW much longer do I have before I've been in 40 minutes?" I kept asking him. I was aware of how numb my fingers and toes were becoming in the freezing lake.

I tried to swim toward the sun, but it was giving me a headache. I found a warm place but banged my knees on the rocks because that spot was only a foot deep. I again swam out where it was deeper, and I was shivering.

"HOW many more minutes?" I badgered Mark. I had promised myself that I'd swim for forty minutes.

"I'm going back up to the car," he said, being saner than I am.

"NO!" I yelled. "Don't leave me here! I'm too cold!"

"Get out of there, then," he said. "You've already been swimming for...." He looked at his watch. "Twenty three minutes."

"That's ALL?" I said. "I feel like I've been in here for weeks!" He began walking up to the car so he could get himself some food from our trip earlier to the Farmer's Market. "How will I know when my time is up?"

"I'll beep the horn," he said. How I longed to be walking up that path again....up to the car...but I had to keep moving. If I stopped at all, I'd begin to shake. Shit. *I need more bulging muscles on my arms and legs,* I thought. *Then I'd be warmer.*

Be mindful, I kept telling myself. Look at the sky! *The water is so....aqua....and fucking freezing! Arghhhh! Beep the horn, damn it!* I silently said to Mark. I watched him as I did every swim stroke I could think of. Backstroke, sidestroke, frog kick, modified breast stroke. My neck was hurting. Everything was hurting. *Be mindful,* I told myself again. But who wants to be mindful when you're in pain?

Then I noticed he was walking towards the car...maybe to beep the horn so I could get out? *No! All he's doing is wandering around and munching on chips, that brat. Eating while I freeze to death! What if I drown? Sometimes people drown when they get too cold. Hypothermia! I'm sure I have hypothermia. I'll probably still be swimming and I'll go into cardiac arrest!*

At long last, he beeped the horn. I galloped out of the water shivering and shaking and was so cold that I couldn't stand still long enough to get my sandals on. So I just ran like I was having a seizure, half falling down and not caring that I was running on dirt and rocks in my bare feet. I was utterly and completely un-mindful, which in the moment, seemed like the far better option. All I wanted was to get into the toasty car and rip off the wet suit (which hadn't done its job) and get my warm clothes on.

When I finally did, I found a patch of sunlight through the trees before the sun went down, and I sat in it and then I faced the sun. Eventually I was able to be mindful—mindful that I had stopped shaking and that mindfulness was not all it was cracked up to be. If the Buddha had ever gone swimming in a lake this cold, he'd understand.

20

SAVING POLLYWOGS

I hated to leave the pollywogs yesterday. They're in a big, almost dried up puddle behind the skating rink at Chavez Community Center, and last week at this time they were swimming merrily around the pond after a couple weeks of rain. But now, the water is almost gone and I'm concerned about them.

This story started one night when I ran into Sam, a young guard I always see at Chavez; he was one of my favorite English 109 students a few years ago. While I was exercising on the elliptical machine, he came up to me and said, "When you're finished here tonight, I want to show you something incredible. I'll be at the front desk." I agreed to meet him, finished up my workout and sweaty as I was, it was a warm night, so we walked out to the path that leads to the back. Almost as soon as we started, I could hear it: this soft sound that filled the night air. It got louder and louder as we got closer, and then I knew what it was: croaking! There were frogs back there! No, Sam corrected me, they're toads. Spadefoot toads.

But when we got to the big pond, I couldn't see anything. He forgot his flashlight so I razzed him about it, but he said even with one, it would be hard to catch sight of the toads. We stood there under the starry sky, and the air vibrated with the hoarse, harsh cries of frogs. The sound was deafening, the best noise in the world.

Excited, I told Mark all about it that night, and a few days later, I brought him over to hear the toads. Since it was daytime, I thought we'd be able to see something. Nothing. He looked at me, wondering what we were doing there, but the toads were asleep, burrowed in the mud. Or possibly, as I found out later, having babies. Turns out that the night the toads were so loud, they were dating. Getting it on.

Two weeks later, Sam told me there were pollywogs back in the pond. "Do you want me to get you some?" he asked. My mind went back to times when I was a kid, catching tadpoles with my friend Tricia Hynes in Hinmen's field where there was mud and dirty water and praying mantises and sun shining on rocks, a place I felt calm and happy with no one to tell me what to do and no worries. I hadn't seen pollywogs in years. How could I say no?

"Of course!" I said. Later he handed me the plastic Coca Cola cup of muddy water and when I lifted up the top, I could see little black, shiny, heads popping up to get air.

"There are about 20 in there," he said, smiling as though happy to have found someone who appreciated pollywogs as much as he did.

I told Mark I had a surprise for him that evening. Then I came home and presented him with the tadpoles. "Aren't they cute?" I asked him.

"What are we going to do with 20 toads?" he asked, but he helped me put them in an open Tupperware container and he scooped up more mud from outdoors, since apparently the tadpoles eat the bacteria in the mud. Next day, he got a terrarium for them, and they began to grow.

We checked out our guide for Southwestern amphibians, and we read that these particular toads grow in seasonal puddles and have an accelerated growth span so they can survive once the puddle dries up.

"Why are they called 'spadefoot toads?'" I asked Mark.

He read to me: "When they're grown, the toads' feet have protrusions on them which help them dig backwards into the mud."

"Their feet are little spades!" I said. "They're survivors, aren't they?" I liked them even more.

Each time I went to Chavez after that, I checked on the tadpoles. They seemed to be swimming happily, even when the water started evaporating around them. At home, the small terrarium on top of my bookcase in the hallway was beginning to stink. The creatures didn't mind if the skin they'd shed was floating around beside them, and we had to leave the muddy water in there because that's their food. But Mark started to complain, so we had to park them in the garage. I thought they'd be OK, except then they became almost motionless. They might have needed more sunlight. But when I shined the flashlight in there, I could see that they had both back and front legs and they were beginning to look more like frogs than fish. After that, I left the light on in the garage.

The following Saturday I went to Chavez even though it was closed for a week because they were renovating. The tadpoles looked to be maturing the same as our garage ones were, and they were still swimming, but most of the pond had disappeared around them so they were in the tiny rivulets. I had brought 4 gallons of rainwater with me, so I poured that on them, thinking they'd be OK for a couple days. But when I went back on Monday, walking gingerly in my good sandals over the muddy little hills that used to be covered with water, the pollywogs were in about 4 or 5 different places, all huddled together on barely wet mud, not moving.

"Oh no!" I yelled and ransacked my car for bottles of drinking water. I found about a gallon's worth and once I poured it on them, they began to move again, a few even beginning to hop with their new little legs. But a lot of them seemed pretty desperate. Even though I was supposed to go back to work that day, I called my boss and told her I had an emergency to take care of. I zoomed to Vitamin Cottage and bought 5 gallons of purified water and then shot back to Chavez and poured it on them. They began to move again, though some seemed beyond help at that point.

Then I called Mark and said he had to do something.

We live in Eldorado, about 20 miles away, but I begged him to bring more rainwater. He said he would; plus he said he'd bring a shovel and dig a little hole for them, a deeper hole full of water that wouldn't evaporate so fast. His mission was successful, and he also brought home another pail of rescued tadpoles that he put outside in a hole next to our rain barrel. It was surrounded by tall weeds, so I hoped the birds wouldn't eat them.

But the situation was urgent; hundreds of tadpoles needed homes or they would die. The next day, I asked my boss at work if she wanted any toads and she looked at me.

"Are you crazy?" she said.

I got on the phone and called Animal Control.

"Hello, can you help me? I need to report that some animals are dying!"

"What animals, Ma'am? Where are these animals?"

"Chavez Community Center. They can't breathe!"

"What happened? I'll have to report this to Dispatch, so I need clear directions on where they are and what their condition is."

"Their water is gone and their legs haven't completely grown in, so they can't hop..."

"Hop?"

"Well, they're toads. That is, they're not toads yet; that's the problem. They're still pollywogs..."

"Pollywogs? You're calling about pollywogs?"

"Yeah, they need oxygen! Or tons more water! Can't you do anything? They're gasping for air! Maybe if you got a fire truck—"

"I'm sorry, Ma'am. We don't have the manpower to deal with pollywogs."

I called Pet Smart next.

"Hello, can Pet Smart save some pollywogs?"

"What are you talking about? Who is this?"

" I'm a customer. I went to your store the other day and I saw frogs there. I have an idea how you can get more frogs for free! There are hundreds of pollywogs at Chavez that are running out of water. If you rescued them...."

"Ma'am, we sell only certified frogs. They have to have papers."

How could they live with themselves?

Maybe I do have some issues with letting go. But as it turned out, Mark and I did save many of the tadpoles that were outdoors at Chavez. Unfortunately, some also died, including most of the ones we'd airlifted to our house. That was a few years ago, and since then, Santa Fe has not had rains like that in September. My guess is that the spade foot toads who survived are waiting underground for the next flood.

Three years later: My postscript to this story is that last week, Mark discovered a spadefoot toad hopping around our driveway one morning after a recent rain. He had no companions, but he did have those telltale protrusions on his back feet so he could dig. He had to be one of our adoptees! Mark caught him and showed him to me, then put him in our garden where there's more water. Soon, hopefully he'll find another survivor like himself and they'll make babies, proving to us that no matter how hard life gets in the desert, if you're a spadefoot toad with friends, you keep going. I know the Buddha didn't believe in getting too attached, but I think he'd have given a compadre some water if he needed it.

21

GOOD GRIEF

After I went to see my Mom for Mother's Day last May, I felt crushed at how she'd declined in the few months since I'd seen her last. She was now having trouble walking, she threw the scrambled eggs I cooked for her across the room, and she hit me on the head when I tried to help her in the bathroom. She was on the road to death and there were no detours.

I went to see the go-to guy for grief in Santa Fe. I had no idea what I was going to say to him, but I knew I had to talk to him first before I could join a Grief Group. He works at the Hospice Center, and after a few minutes waiting, I was ushered back to his office.

"What can I do for you?" he asked. He was a slightly built middle aged man with graying hair.

"My mother's really sick and she's 91," I said. "I can't believe how much worse she is, now. She called me a shithead last time I saw her. I mean she has Alzheimer's...." I started to cry. He let me carry on for a long time, using up half his Kleenex box before I stopped.

"I'm sorry," he said.

"I'm angry too!" I yelled. "I don't even know who God is, or if there is a God! Why is this happening to my mother?"

"That's a normal feeling," he said. He's a very calm person.

"But no one wants to hear about my mother!" I said. "That's why I need to get into a Grief Group!"

"Getting anger out is important," he said. "Elizabeth Kubler Ross suggested that her clients use rubber pipe and whack it against the wall to express their frustration."

"She did?" That made me feel a little bit better, though I wondered where to buy the rubber pipe. "But can I get into a group?"

"Well, in order to join one of our groups, you have to have lost someone very close to you, to death. And your mother, well, she does sound like she isn't going to be around much longer, but....is she in Hospice?"

"No!" I said. "She's not really dying. I mean, not yet, not actively..."

"That's a problem," he said.

"But my cat is pretty sick," I offered. "She's almost 18 yrs. old and has a lot of kidney problems..."

"I'm sorry," he said.

"You mean I need an actual dead person to get in a Grief group?" I handed him back the Kleenex box.

He smiled. "Well, I wouldn't put it that way, but yes." We sat in silence for a minute or two.

"Actually, my good friend died three months ago," I said. "But he wasn't a member of my family."

"Were you very close to him?" he asked.

"I was! We'd been friends for 14 years. Not as long as my relationship with my cat, but...." I sniffed.

"That might work." He gave me a few handouts about various grief groups in town, and we shook hands on it. I had to figure out which one would fit my schedule, but I was eager to get started, so as soon as I walked out to the parking lot, I got on my cell phone and left messages for as many grief counselors as I had numbers for.

"My mother is 91 and very sick with Alzheimer's," I said. "And my cat is sick. I also have a close friend who died in February. Can I join your group?"

No one answered that night, though I was in a grief-group mood. I had already expressed my feelings that day, and I thought I'd be excellent at explaining myself to strangers if I had the chance. But none of the counselors picked up.

As the days passed though, I kept getting calls on my cell at the most inopportune times from these grief counselors. There I'd be at Albertson's, in line carrying bags of produce and a greasy roast chicken, and my phone would ring. If I could put my things down on the counter, I would pick up.

"Hello, this is Madeline DeRose, is this Terry?"

"Yes?"

"I run the Grief group at St. Vincent's and I wanted to know if you're OK. Tell me how you're feeling; you're not suicidal, are you?"

Then I realized my speaker phone was on and the people behind me were giving me strange looks. One woman in front of me dropped her parsnips.

But after a few weeks of this, I settled on a Grief group that met at St. Francis Cathedral on Tuesday evenings. I didn't know what to expect, but it helped that the head honcho of the group was a nun, Sister Denise. Not that I have completely positive feelings about nuns, but they were a familiar breed, and her voice sounded kind.

The first night I attended, I had trouble finding parking, so I was a few minutes late. This older woman in a skirt and blouse was waving at me, so I followed her into the building. I suppose she could have been an axe murderer, but she turned out to be Sister Denise, a nun in plainclothes. The Big Kahuna of Grief on Tuesday nights at the Cathedral.

I sat down in a circle of folding chairs and I was asked to introduce myself and why I was there. I began with a story about my sick mother, then continued about my ailing cat. But when Sister Denise glared at me, I explained that my good friend Jim had died just a few months before. Everyone sighed with relief. I guess a woman who had lost only a beloved dog had come to the group recently, but she had to be thrown out because she hadn't lost an actual person.

As the weeks of the summer went by slowly, I attended

every Tuesday night. I realized Sister was skilled at what she did. Her previous job was as a counselor at Bernardinelli's Funeral Home, so she knew a lot about ashes. She loved to say, "They're not 'REmains,' they're 'CREmains!'" She'd tell us about bone fragments and pieces of elbow that might be in the cremains. When she talked like this, I didn't want to listen. Usually the stories were sad in that group, but a dark humor emerged. Like one guy was talking about finding his father in a pool of blood, dead on the front walk. Other members of the group were silent, listening and respectful, but Hilda, an old woman who wasn't hearing everything, interrupted in a loud voice.

"I love your glasses!" she yelled to me. "Where did you buy them?"

And then Sister had to say, "Hilda, we LISTEN when others are speaking!"

Hilda in her 80's, who had skinny legs and dirty white ankle socks and a couple scabs on her knees, talked about her dead sisters.

There were times I cried my eyes out in the group, talking about Jim, livid at God. One woman tried to comfort me, saying that when she sees pennies on the ground, she feels her dead parents are trying to communicate. But pennies don't help me. Sometimes in the group, if someone was rambling on, not emoting enough, Sister Denise (who had the five stages of grief tattooed on her brain) would get right up in the person's face:

"Are you feeling ANGER? Let it out! Are you bargaining? Get into acceptance!"

❦

Five weeks into the group, my 18 year old cat died. I loved my little cat, Butch; she'd been my friend for so long. My husband was out of town working at the time, and I couldn't decide whether to bury her on our land or have her cremated. It was late on a Sunday night, and I felt lost. I realized I had questions about cremation. Then that line from Ghostbusters occurred to me: "Who ya gonna call?"

Of course I called Sister Denise; she knew everything about death and what to do afterwards. I pictured her having an office at St. Francis Cathedral and I'd just leave her a message.

"Hello?" a sleepy voice answered.

Shit! I thought. Shit! I almost hung up, but then I thought, *Well, Jeez, she is the expert on this. I've already woken her up....*

"I'm sorry, Sister, I thought you had an office and I was going to leave you a voicemail because my cat died today! Should I cremate her or bury her?"

"What time is it?" she asked. "Lord of God, it's 2:30 am!"

"I didn't mean to wake you. But 'cremation' is your middle name!" She yawned and then talked to me for a few minutes.

After that night, she didn't seem to like me as well. She never called on me first in the group, more like third or fourth. I had decided not to follow her advice; I'd buried Butch in our backyard.

Then about a week later, an unsympathetic soul from work told me I needed to get over my cat, that I should just imagine her marching into Animal Heaven. She kind of yelled at me, so I phoned Sister Denise about it.

"I'd been feeling good that I buried Butch out back," I began. "But then this woman..."

"When is your husband coming back home?" was the first thing out of Sister's mouth.

Right after Mark returned from his work in Australia though, he got a very serious case of pneumonia. He was hospitalized twice and very ill, so I needed to be with him all the time. I didn't have time to attend the group anymore, but Sister Denise put us on her prayer list and called me periodically to see if he was getting better. I decided she had a very good heart; I just needed to call her the right time of the day.

What did I learn from all this? That when someone dies, you need understanding people to talk to. I also learned that a dead cat and a sick mother won't get you into a grief group. And nuns don't have answering machines.

Mainly though, I just listen to Sweet Honey in the Rock sing their gorgeous song, "Breaths."

Those who have died, have never really left; the dead are not under the earth.

They are in the groaning rocks, they are in the air we breathe. The dead have a pact with the living...

22

BLUE

I remember blue, the Blessed Virgin in our backyard who rose up out of the fog and lighted on the clothesline like a dragonfly with huge blue wings. She was beautiful I remember, and so free of sadness, so kind. She floated for awhile before she landed and I recall thinking she may have worried whether the clothespoles could hold her. I watched out my bedroom window, where I'd expected to see only poplar trees there standing in a row like soldiers, but then a blue vapor began to form to the left, and there she was.

The day I saw her, I was in my room because I'd had a fight with my father. Just when I thought he was going to be the sweet and funny father I loved so much, his face got red and angry and he roared as though he hated me. He'd yelled that I'd awakened him from a sound sleep as he lay in bed behind his white door although I hadn't meant to. I ran for the refuge of my bedroom with those dust balls like clouds under my double bed and I laid on the orange bedspread upside down so I could watch our yard, how the poplar trees protected me.

That yard was my solace, the raspberry bushes that brambled at the back and called me to explore them, the pear tree where I buried my dead pets, the crabapple tree that I climbed to heaven. I could lie in that tall wet grass and watch animals gallop across the sky. Just looking at the yard gave me hope. And then I saw her, the holy one who my mother said only appeared to saints or sheepherder children in Fatima. The stone statue of her that I always wished would smile at me in Church was now coming in for a landing in our backyard! But only because I was watching; and it wasn't her statue, it was her: real yet filmy like my mother's nylon stockings. I don't remember everything about her because her body was indistinct, but her face held so much love for me that I forgot all about my father's fury.

Later, I told my mother my secret and she said I was imagining things; my vision wasn't real. But I knew the Blessed Virgin was there because I needed her and she promised with her eyes to never leave me. And even though I never saw her in the same way again, her mist was there in an afterglow. Whenever I felt as lost as I did that day, all I had to do was look out that dirty bedroom window, the one with the broken sash, and I saw a blue haze. Then I knew she was watching me and praying with me. After that, my father couldn't sting me so much anymore because I had the secret of knowing I would never be alone, not really. I found out that day that sometimes one person can really upset me, but then something else so unexpected happens like a blue jay landing in my hand or sunlight surprising me on my face. Then I remember how things are supposed to be.

Acknowledgments

I would like to thank the many friends, family members and colleagues who have helped me over the years to become a better writer and a better person. There are too many therapists to name but you know who you are. Special thanks go to those who have helped me put this book together including Miriam Sagan, Sean Murphy, and to Natalie Goldberg for her influence on my approach to writing and that of so many others. And special love to my husband, Mark Friedman, for always supporting me, for getting every joke, and for nagging me till I finished this book.

"Don't I Know You from Way Back" was published in *The Eldorado Sun* (2007).

"Socks" was published in the *Santa Fe Literary Review* (2008).

"Half-Naked Surfing" was published in the *Santa Fe Reporter* (2003).

"Why Can't They Let Us Be Beautiful?" was published in *Crosswinds Weekly* (2000).

19654094R00069

Made in the USA
Charleston, SC
05 June 2013